Chris Benians
The Collection, London

Barney Brown
Betelnut, San Francisco

Peter Gordon
The Sugar Club, London

Graham Harris
Cicada, London

Michael Lee-Richards
Michael's, Christchurch

Charles Phan
The Slanted Door, San Francisco

Stanislaus Soares
Chinois, Melbourne

Chef Suki
Masons, San Francisco

Cass Titcombe
The Collection, London

Kirk Webber
Cafe Kati, San Francisco

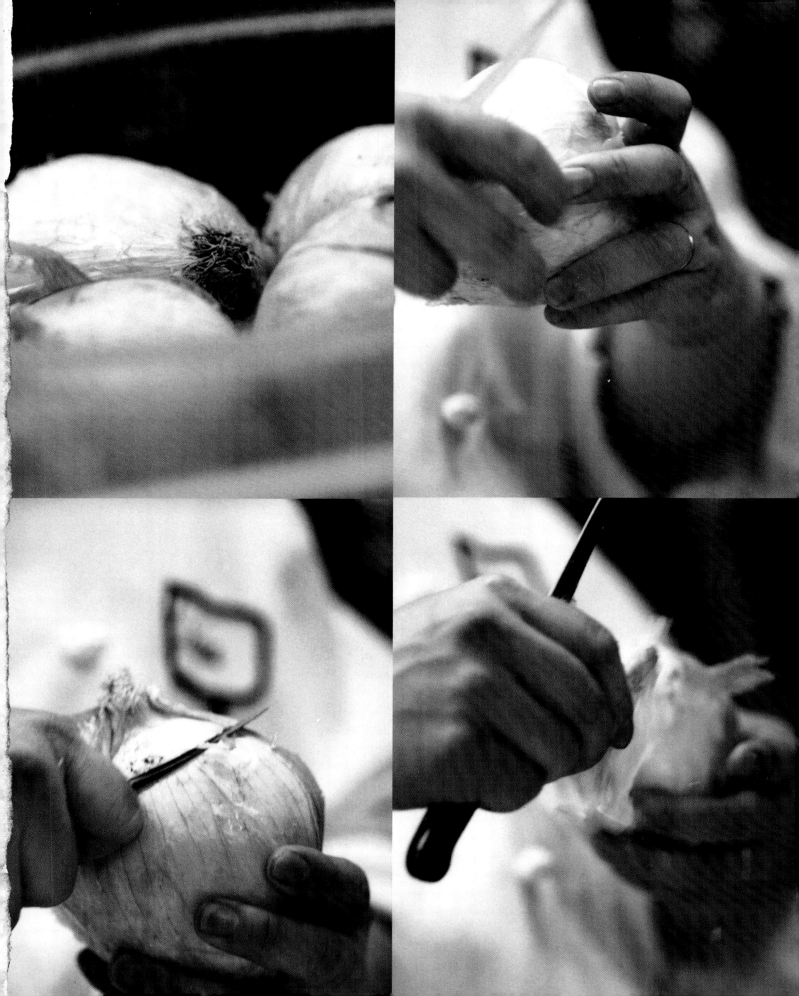

Food is an explosion of energy, stimulation and inspiration. This is an investigation of flavors that excite the palate and encourage further discovery.

east west food

edited by Sasha Judelson
photography by Sandra Lane

SOMA
san francisco

the influences

First published 1997 by Hamlyn, an imprint of Reed Books Limited. This North American edition published 1997 by SOMA Books, by arrangement with Hamlyn / Reed Books Limited.

SOMA Books may be purchased for educational, business, or sales promotional use at attractive quantity discounts. Please contact Bay Books & Tapes / 555 De Haro St., No. 220 / San Francisco, CA 94107.

Library of Congress Cataloging-in-Publication Data: East West food / edited by Sasha Judelson ; photography by Sandra Lane. p. cm. Includes index. ISBN 1-57959-002-0 (hardcover) 1. Cookery, International. 2. Cookery, Oriental. I. Judelson, Sasha. TX725.A1E25   1997 641.59--dc21   97-30191 CIP

Printed and bound in China
10 9 8 7 6 5 4 3 2 1

SOMA / South of Market Books
is an imprint of Bay Books & Tapes.
For SOMA Books:
Publisher: James Connolly
Editorial Director: Pamela Byers
Art Director: Jeffrey O'Rourke
North American Copy Editor: Sharon Silva

For Hamlyn:
Publishing Director: Laura Bamford
Senior Editor: Sasha Judelson
Assistant Editor: Katey Day
Art Director: Keith Martin
Senior Designer: Louise Leffler
Photographer: Sandra Lane
Interviews and additional text: Sasha Judelson

ISBN 1-57959-002-0
Distributed to the trade by Publishers Group West

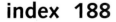

"I think of it as my journey of food. In 30 years I have worked in Russia, Finland, Sweden, Norway, Britain, Germany, France, New York, Miami, Houston, many, many places, and I have picked up elements from all over."

Chef Suki, chef at Masons, San Francisco

introduction
what is East-West food?

In the very simplest of terms, it is the fusion of flavors and techniques from both the West and the East. But this is not a simple concept, mostly because there are so many variations in the interpretation of East-West food. It is, in fact, the diversification that makes this style of cooking so exciting.

To look at the concept in a little more detail makes it easier to understand. It also means that we can be clearer as to why it has happened. If a Chinese, Japanese or any Southeast Asian chef starts to cook in Europe, America or any Western country, they will find the ingredients that they are able to buy in this new location are not the same as in their native country. Neither are the cooking styles or techniques most commonly used. The same will happen if an American, European or Australian cooks in a different culture. What they are used to finding readily available may no longer be that easy to find.

So chefs and cooks alike adapt their dishes and approach. On the whole though, they do not lose all the elements of what they know – they simply adapt them to suit what is at hand. It is more than likely that the dishes will not be exactly the same as they had been, but they will be similar. They are the same basic ideas. As with all things, a little successful experimentation gives us all the confidence to continue investigating. So, as the barriers are pushed a bit further, more blending takes place.

Having jumped any initial boundaries, it is easier to continue the process of exploration. In this way, we find global fusion: food that has flavors and influences from various parts of the world. This does not have to be food from everywhere on one plate!

It is infinitely more successful if the combinations come from a knowledge of the flavors. It is not really possible to build on food if one doesn't understand the

"Over the years I have been at Chinois, I have refined, reworked and extended the influences to incorporate the best of Australian, Asian and Eastern flavors."

Stanislaus Soares, chef at Chinois, Melbourne

> "If chefs don't understand the basis of cooking, how can they do a twist on it? It you don't know how to make puff pastry, you can't make a variation of puff pastry."
>
> Kirk Webber, chef at Cafe Kati, San Francisco

> "Fusion food has happened because of the invention of the jet plane and subsequent massive movement of human beings across the planet, and the fact that they brought their taste buds with them. Then adapting to the availability of ingredients and the different local produce and new ways of cooking. You do fusion food because you can."
>
> Michael Lee-Richards, chef at Michael's, Christchurch

basics. After all, these have come from years of experience and forethought, which is partly why they have continued in the repertoire.

The best way forward is therefore to build on a solid basis. Each chef begins from a different starting point: what food they grew up on, how their mother, father even grandparents cooked, where they grew up, their own likes and dislikes, and so on. These various influences add to the vast umbrella under which East-West food rests.

East-West food is more than an absorption and blending of food and techniques, because it can be looked at from so many different angles and taken in so many different ways. A further understanding of food and techniques can lead to a desire to look at the possibilities of a single ingredient, or a coalition of ingredients. It might be that, as a cook, you find a particular union mouthwatering, and you know that taking one element of that union and putting it with another will also work. Most chefs and cooks will agree that this whole process is one of experimentation, seeing what works and enjoying the discovery. It relies on knowing sweet and sour, the various textures, fish, meat, poultry and game and the huge variety of fruits and vegetables that exist; on knowing how to balance the foods and build the dish.

So why has this cross-culturalization of food happened? The answer is that there are many different reasons. More people are able to travel farther afield, so enjoying the opportunity to experience a wider range of foods. There has been an explosion of food coverage in the media, newspapers, magazines and the television, and the retail industry has responded to the demand created by this enlivened interest. An ever-growing range of products is available at supermarkets and other stores, the equipment and utensils are easier to find, and we experience this style of food at more and more restaurants. Which brings us back full circle to the opportunity. As new foods, techniques and styles are absorbed into our culture, so they become the norm.

As said, the food, dishes and menus that evolve as a result of experimentation depend on a depth of knowledge. They all have a strong basis, which is why this book is structured by influences. These influences are all principle factors in the creation of fusion and cross-cultural food. Take them how you like, and there are of course others, but Asia and the Pacific, the wok, noodles, chilies, rice, citrus fruits, herbs and spices, fish, fast food

"A lot of care and love has gone into the creation of various types of food and I carry those concepts with me and bring them to Vietnamese food. The local ingredient dictates the direction, and the Vietnamese tradition dictates the taste of cooking. But I'm not just carelessly throwing things together."

Charles Phan, chef at The Slanted Door, San Francisco

"We ended up as a collection of food, as a little bit from here and little from there and a little bit from there."

Cass Titcombe, chef at The Collection, London

are all determinants: they can make the difference.

As a continent, Asia has, in the last 20 years, seen people take a great deal more interest in it. In some respects, the Pacific is a contrast to Asia, which is what many of us see as the Pacific Rim. It therefore brings in some of the elements that do not naturally fall into Asian cuisine. The blending process works both ways: it is chefs from both of these defined areas who take some direction from the other area. Using relatively newly found foods and techniques is a greater challenge than simply sticking to their own well-known sources.

Cooking in a wok is fast, but it is not really fast-food because it does not have the same connotations. To cook in a wok one needs to be aware of its various qualities

"We do put restrictions on ourselves, there are certain things we won't do. We won't put olive oil with anything Asian."

Chris Benians, chef at The Collection, London

"There is a process chefs go through when putting a dish together; they don't just throw it on a plate. They first think about the combinations and what ingredients they want to use, then the flavors they're looking for and if they'll work together, and of course how it will look on the plate; then they will probably try the dish at home first, perhaps cook it for friends and work colleagues. If the dish works they will put it on the menu, so you can see, even chefs don't get it right the first time."

Graham Harris, chef at Cicada, London

and possibilities. There are rudimentary points to using a wok and knowing them clearly helps. And when you know them you can, once again, build on them.

Chilies just fire the imagination, and they can easily turn a dish around from, perhaps, something ordinary into something altogether different. There are literally hundreds of varieties of chili, all subtly different from one another. Finding out how to use them, in what, when and where is great fun just to start.

Noodles and rice are basic starches so they can be a good first layer to a dish. But, they can be much more as well: they both make good accompaniments, they are wonderful key elements, and, they work well as the main player in a dish. Citrus fruits add zest, tang and a sharp flavor. Herbs and spices, too, are decisive elements, because their flavors are distinct and can alter a dish.

Fish is crucial to this food because there is such a huge variety of it, it readily takes on flavorings and can be cooked in many different ways. Additionally, the nutritional qualities of fish are broadly known nowadays, and that makes it more a appealing ingredient to cook.

Fast food we all know, and some of us love it more than others. The important thing is that it has a huge impact, and the brief time factor is a reason alone to take it seriously. This time rationale motivates us all at some point: we're hungry and want to eat, but many of us want to eat well, too. To bring together the two elements of desire – fast and delicious – is close to perfection.

Obviously various different cultures have had an impact on this food development as well, but, their impression is less easy to define and assimilate. That does not mean that it is any less important. The delicacies and intricacies of individual cuisines are a crucial part of this advancement of food.

Having structured the book by influence, this arrangement is augmented by the recipes and thoughts that have come from the chefs. These chefs work in restaurants around the world: London, San Francisco, Christchurch and Melbourne. Each chef has his individual take on food. Independence of ideas is fundamental to the success of this type of food. The chefs' recipes set out to show how they create their dishes, and their comments and recipe introductions expand upon this. Try the dishes or change them, too, if you wish to create your own fusion food. Don't be put off if you cannot find all the exact ingredients specified. It is the essence of the flavors that is important, so take that as your principal element and adapt it if you need or want to. Start off by following the principle of knowing the basics: cook the recipes as specified before you experiment with the ideas. Exercise that good judgment, which is integral to creating good food. Above all, enjoy the inspiration that this book sets out to provide.

Fusion food, cross-cultural food, Pacific Rim cooking, mixed food or whatever guise it comes under is there to be enjoyed. Essentially, it is a natural succession to the food of before. It is not readily defined, but that is the nature of it: it is made up from many different elements. None of the chefs who have chosen to take up this sort of food have slotted themselves into a straitjacket, but rather they have taken their inspiration from what is around now, what influences they know and those they have picked up, both previously and currently. Attitudes alter and so a chance to change opens up, and *East West Food* explores that opportunity to inspire and stimulate us all. This is exciting food – not difficult, somewhat new and possibly unknown – but delicious, mouthwatering and wonderful.

"I'd like to do a little more changing because you tend to become stagnant if you do the same thing over and over, but I would like to make everything perfect so we can do things with our hands tied behind our back and then go on to the next level after that."

Barney Brown, chef at Betelnut, San Francisco

"Some people say that the term 'fusion' sounds technical and the food itself isn't. For me, a good cook can combine the technical with a more esoteric feeling for food, and the latter is the harder of the two to teach."

Peter Gordon, chef at The Sugar Club, London

Asian-Pacific food

Asian-Pacific comes partly from Asia and partly from the Pacific.

Asian-Pacific food is a combination of food inspired by the techniques and flavors of both the countries that make up Asia and the countries that border on the Pacific Ocean. Asia and the Pacific are the two most fundamental influences on this cuisine; Europe and Australia come into it as well. This is food that we recognize, with an extra lift. Well-known dishes are given additional complementary flavors, and taste buds are pushed a little further than usual.

Asian-Pacific food is not easily categorized because this food has a wide spectrum, being made up of a number of different elements. When creating Asian-Pacific food, any chef or cook will always want to ensure that all of the elements are complementary, something which is made easier by a depth of knowledge and by using the distinctive flavors of foods that are native to Asia and the Pacific. Using lesser known ingredients adds an element of differentiation to a dish; using those same ingredients together with better known ingredients leads to a hint of familiarity and so to an easy acceptance.

Asian-Pacific food can be eclectic, and is always stimulating. It is a combination that brings together a diversity of styles, and it is easily accepted because our knowledge of food is growing ever greater. This knowledge and the availability of ingredients enables any cook to transform their own well known dishes, which may mean that they now include these recently found ingredients. However it evolves, food from Asia and the Pacific is always fascinating – and tantalizing to the palate.

"In Southeast Asian cooking there are some wonderful combinations and by adding, say, a third ingredient it changes completely, or by removing another ingredient it changes completely. A lot of the combinations are interchangeable almost, but we do like to

keep it interesting. Sweet and sour, salty, sometimes you can get five or six different flavors in one dish."

Barney Brown, chef at Betelnut

"At The Collection we serve this dish with a garnish of julienned orange sweet potatoes, which are deep-fried until crisp and then drained. You could also make this dish with salmon, halibut or swordfish."

Sesame-Crusted Tuna

1. Whisk the egg white with half the soy sauce and brush over one side of each tuna steak. Cover the coated side with the sesame seeds, making sure there are none on the outsides of the fish. Set aside.

2. Purée the red chili pepper with the garlic, ginger and shallot in 2 tablespoons of the sunflower oil. Process until almost smooth.

3. Heat half of the remaining oil in a heavy sauté pan until very hot. Add the tuna steaks, sesame side down, reduce the heat slightly and cook the tuna for about 2 minutes or until the seeds have formed a golden crust over the tuna. Turn the steaks over and cook for about 2 minutes longer for rare (increase the cooking time if you prefer the tuna well done). Transfer to a platter and keep warm.

4. While the tuna is cooking, heat a wok until very hot. Add the remaining oil, then the bok choy stalks and some of the chili purée, depending on how spicy you like your food.

5. Stir-fry this mixture for about 2 minutes, then add the shredded bok choy leaves, together with the lime juice and the remaining soy sauce. Cook for about 1 minute longer, then divide the mixture among four plates. Top the bok choy with a tuna steak and accompany each serving with a wedge of lime.

Serves 4

Chris Benians and Cass Titcombe at The Collection

1 egg white

¼ cup soy sauce

four 5-ounce blue fin tuna steaks, about ¾ inch thick

⅔ cup sesame seeds

1 red chili pepper, seeded

2 garlic cloves

1-inch piece ginger root, peeled

1 small shallot

4 tablespoons sunflower oil

4 small bok choy, stalks chopped and leaves shredded

2 limes, 1 juiced and 1 cut into quarters

Blue Cheese, Avocado
and Shrimp Sushi

2 cups Japanese short-grain rice

2½ cups water

4 tablespoons French dressing

3½ ounces blue cheese, crumbled

7 ounces peeled cooked shrimp,
    finely chopped

salt and pepper, to taste

2 avocados

juice of 1 lemon

nori sheets

NORI

Nori is a type of seaweed, mainly used for wrapping sushi. It is sold in very thin sheets. To toast nori, simply grill on one side. It can also be crisped in the oven and, if preferred, brushed with oil before toasting.

1. Place the rice and the measured water in a saucepan and bring to a boil. As soon as the water comes to a boil, cover the pan with the lid and reduce the heat to the lowest setting for 20 minutes.

2. Turn off the heat and allow the rice to stand in the saucepan, still covered, for 10 minutes longer. Remove the lid and cover the pan with a clean tea towel and stand for a further 10 minutes.

3. Gently fold the dressing, cheese, shrimp and some black pepper into the rice (add the dressing gradually to prevent the rice from becoming too wet). Add salt to taste and set aside to cool.

4. Meanwhile, peel, pit and finely dice the avocados. Toss with the lemon juice to stop any discoloring.

5. Lay one nori sheet on a sushi mat. Spread the rice over the nori, then scatter some of the avocado along one edge. Roll up the nori tightly and set aside. Continue until all the mixture is used up.

6. Chill until ready to serve, then cut across into cylindrical pieces and serve on a platter or on individual plates.

Serves 6–8

Michael Lee-Richards at Michael's

GRAVLAX (also spelt gravadlax)

Originating from Sweden, traditional gravlax is salmon that is cured with salt, sugar and dill. In the conventional method it marinates for 2–3 days, and it is the flavor of dill that comes through.

Wasabi Bavarois
with Spiced Gravlax and Sake

1. Beat the eggs in a large bowl just until foamy then set aside. Dissolve the gelatin in ½ cup of the water.

2. Add the gelatin to the eggs with the sugar, 6 tablespoons of the water, the vinegar and Tabasco.

3. In a small bowl, blend the wasabi, turmeric and salt in the remaining water. Stir into the egg mixture and heat gently in a double boiler until thoroughly blended and dissolved, stirring all the time.

4. Remove from the double boiler and stir until cool. Fold in the cream and pour the mixture into one large or four small individual molds that have been rinsed out with water. Chill for at least 2 hours before serving.

5. Rinse the salmon fillet and pat dry. Brush the fish with the sake. Combine the salt and sugar with all the spices and rub all over both sides of the salmon.

6. Place the rubbed salmon in a stainless steel, glass or ceramic dish. Lay the orange and lemon slices over the top of the fish, alternating the different slices.

7. Cover the fish with plastic wrap and refrigerate for about 48 hours.

8. To serve, turn the bavarois out on to a large white platter or individual plates. Arrange the thinly sliced gravlax to one side and garnish with salad greens. Dust the edge of the plate with a little wasabi powder.

Serves 6

Michael Lee-Richards at Michael's

4 eggs

1 tablespoon unflavored gelatin

1 cup water

1 cup sugar

½ cup cider vinegar

4 drops Tabasco sauce

2 tablespoons wasabi powder, plus a little for dusting

½ teaspoon ground turmeric

¼ teaspoon salt

1-1½ cups heavy cream

salad greens, to garnish

Spiced Gravlax

1 large salmon fillet, tiny bones removed

1 tablespoon sake

1 cup salt

1 cup brown sugar

1 teaspoon ground cilantro

1 teaspoon ground allspice

1 teaspoon ground cloves

¼ cup peppercorns, crushed

1 tablespoon crushed dried chili peppers

2 large oranges, thinly sliced

4 lemons, thinly sliced

"In one restaurant we have lots of different flavors, but without fighting. Global fusion food flavors never fight each other."

Chef Suki, chef at Masons

"My food is fairly in your face in terms of flavor. I like good, earthy food, tasty meats, solid combinations and robust presentation. I wouldn't regard myself as subtle, though goodness knows, I try!"

Michael Lee-Richards, chef at Michael's

Roasted Tomato Soup with Yogurt

1. Preheat the oven to 350°F. Cut the tomatoes lengthwise in half and brush with 2 tablespoons of the oil and 1 tablespoon of the honey. Place the tomatoes, cut side up, in a large roasting pan and roast in the oven for 1½ hours or until caramelized and slightly dehydrated. If time permits bake at 225°F for 6 hours.

2. Heat the remaining oil in a large saucepan. Add the onion, garlic and tom yum paste and cook, stirring frequently to make sure that the mixture does not scorch.

3. Add the roasted tomatoes with the tomato juice and remaining honey. Bring to a boil, then reduce the heat and simmer for about 5 minutes.

4. To serve, taste and adjust the seasoning and honey, if necessary. Ladle into bowls and garnish with yogurt and a little more tom yum paste.

Serves 6

Michael Lee-Richards at Michael's

4 pounds ripe tomatoes

6 tablespoons grapeseed or light olive oil

2 tablespoons clear honey, plus extra to taste

1 large onion, finely chopped

4 garlic cloves, finely chopped

2 teaspoons tom yum paste, or to taste, plus extra for garnishing

6 cups tomato juice or V8 juice

salt and pepper, to taste

yogurt, to garnish

TOM YUM

Tom yum is a thin, brown and red paste with a hot and sour taste. It is mostly used to make a Thai soup of the same name. Lemongrass is one of the ingredients in the paste, and the taste of that herb comes through.

Vietnamese Peanut Wontons
with Red Curry Sauce

8 green onions, finely chopped

6 tablespoons lemon juice

2 small red chili peppers, seeded and
   finely chopped

5 tablespoons superfine sugar

1½ cups coarsely ground roasted peanuts

¼–½ teaspoon salt

½–1 cup fresh white bread crumbs

1 package wonton wrappers

oil for deep-frying

Red Curry Dipping Sauce

1 tablespoon sesame oil

4 green onions, finely chopped

1 tablespoon Thai red curry paste

1½ cups canned coconut milk

1 tablespoon light soy sauce

1. Start by making the dipping sauce. Heat the oil in a sauté pan. Add the green onions, and cook, stirring, for about 1 minute. Stir in the curry paste and cook for 1 minute longer. Pour in the coconut milk and bring the mixture to a boil. Reduce the heat and simmer for about 15 minutes or until reduced by half and thickened. Stir in the soy sauce and allow the mixture to cool slightly.

2. Meanwhile, in a small bowl, combine the green onions with the lemon juice, chopped red chili peppers, superfine sugar, roasted peanuts and salt. Taste for seasoning.

3. Stir in some of the fresh bread crumbs, adding just enough to bind the mixture together.

4. Lay the wonton wrappers on the work surface. Brush each generously with water and place a teaspoon of the green onion mixture in the center of each wrapper. Pull the sides of the wrappers in and twist them together to form a long handle for the wonton.

5. Heat the oil in a deep frying pan or deep-fat fryer to 350–375°F, or until a cube of bread browns in 30 seconds. Working in small batches, drop the wontons into the hot oil and fry until golden brown all over. Transfer to a baking sheet lined with paper towels and keep warm in a low oven. These wontons will hold well and they can be made well in advance and reheated, but they are always much better when served as soon as they are cooked.

6. Serve the wontons on large trays, with a bowl of the dipping sauce to one side.

Serves 6–8

Michael Lee-Richards at Michael's

Root Vegetable Curry
with Green Peppercorn Meringue

4 tablespoons olive oil

3 red onions, cut into wedges

4 cups diced blanched root vegetables,
   such as carrots, potatoes and parsnips

1 cup diced celery and carrots

4 garlic cloves, finely chopped

1 pound fresh tomatoes, seeded and coarsely
   chopped

1 cup sun-dried tomatoes, coarsely chopped

3 tablespoons tomato paste

1¾ cups canned coconut milk

¾ cup grated Parmesan cheese

salt and pepper, to taste

Curry Base

1 teaspoon ground cilantro

1 teaspoon ground turmeric

1 teaspoon paprika

½ teaspoon ground cumin

½ teaspoon cayenne pepper

½ teaspoon ground ginger

Meringue

4 egg whites

pinch cream of tartar

pinch salt

1 cup superfine sugar

½ cup water

2 tablespoons green peppercorns

1. Heat half the oil in a large sauté pan. Add the onions and cook, stirring, for about 5 minutes until soft and slightly browned. Using a slotted spoon, transfer the onions to a plate and keep warm.

2. Heat the remaining oil in the pan. Add the root vegetables and sauté until lightly browned. Add to the plate.

3. In a bowl, combine all the ingredients for the curry base. Stir the mixture into the sauté pan together with the diced carrots, celery and garlic and cook, stirring frequently, for about 5 minutes.

4. Add the fresh and sun-dried tomatoes, tomato paste and coconut milk, stirring well. Bring to a boil, then reduce the heat and simmer the mixture gently until the tomatoes have broken down, a thick sauce has formed and the flavors have intensified.

5. Return the onions and root vegetables to the pan and stir into the sauce. Simmer gently for about 15 minutes or until all the vegetables are very soft. Season to taste. Remove from the heat and keep warm while making the green peppercorn meringue.

6. Make the meringue. Lightly whisk the egg whites with the cream of tartar and salt, until frothy.

7. Combine the sugar with the measured water and peppercorns in a small saucepan and bring slowly to a boil. Boil for 4 minutes, then remove from the heat.

8. Whisk the egg whites for a few minutes longer until soft peaks form. Slowly pour the peppercorn syrup into the egg whites while still whisking, and continue to whisk for about 15 seconds longer to mix thoroughly.

9. Preheat the oven to 375°F. Transfer the vegetable curry to an ovenproof dish and sprinkle with half the Parmesan cheese. Pile the meringue mixture over the top and then dust with the remaining Parmesan cheese. Bake the dish in the hot oven until cooked and lightly browned, about 20 minutes. Serve at once.

Serves 4

Michael Lee-Richards at Michael's

Grilled Ahi Tuna Steak
on Asian Risotto

AHI TUNA

Ahi is a Hawaiian term for tuna that is widely used throughout the United States. The tuna to which it refers is not necessarily from Hawaii, but it will be from the Pacific.

1. Start by making the sauce. In a wide saucepan, sauté the shallots and garlic in a little of the oil until translucent. Stir in the white wine and bay leaf. Simmer until reduced by about half. Add the tomato paste, chicken and veal stocks and the lemon juice. Simmer until reduced to a thick sauce. Add the basil and butter and season to taste with salt and pepper.

2. Cook the Japanese rice in boiling water according to the packet instructions. In 1 tablespoon of the oil, sauté the Chinese sausage until browned and the shiitake mushrooms until softened. Add the sherry, oyster sauce, soy sauce, sautéed Chinese sausage, mushrooms, water chestnuts and green onions to the rice.

3. In your hands, form the rice mixture into four 2-inch round patties. Coat them in the couscous.

4. Heat the remaining 2 tablespoons of oil in a wide frying pan and sauté the rice patties until golden all over. Top with the Fontina cheese and cook a few minutes longer until melted. Transfer to a plate lined with paper towels and keep warm in a low oven.

5. Wrap the smoked shrimp in the shiso leaves. Combine the measured ice water with the beaten egg and mix thoroughly. Add the flour gradually, using a fork to incorporate it into the liquid, but being careful not to overmix. Dip the wrapped shrimp in the batter and then fry them over high heat.

6. Cut the tuna into eight medallions. Season with salt and pepper and brush with olive oil.

7. Prepare a fire in a grill or preheat a broiler. Grill or broil the tuna medallions until cooked rare.

8. To serve, place a risotto cake in the center of each of four plates. Place two of the shiso shrimp just behind the risotto cake, with some of the sautéd leeks. Lay two of the tuna medallions in front of the risotto cake. Pour the sauce to the side of the tuna and place the carrots and haricots verts around the plate.

Serves 4

Chef Suki at Masons

1½ pounds ahi tuna, center cut from loin
salt and pepper, to taste
olive oil, for brushing

Herb Tomato Sauce with Garlic Butter

2 shallots, chopped
2 garlic cloves, finely chopped
1 tablespoon olive oil
2 tablespoons dry white wine
½ bay leaf
½ cup tomato paste
¼ cup chicken stock
¼ cup veal stock
1 tablespoon lemon juice
1 teaspoon basil, finely shredded
1 teaspoon butter
salt and pepper, to taste

Rice

⅔ cup Japanese short-grain rice
3 tablespoons vegetable oil
4 ounces lop chony (Chinese sweet sausage), sliced
2 ounces shiitake mushrooms
2 tablespoons medium-dry sherry
2 tablespoons oyster sauce
2 tablespoons soy sauce
½ cup sliced water chestnuts
⅔ cup sliced green onions
⅓ cup couscous
4 slices Fontina cheese

Smoked Shiso Shrimp

16 large smoked shrimp, deveined and halved
8 fresh shiso leaves, halved
⅔ cup ice water
1 egg, beaten
⅔ cup all-purpose flour

Vegetables (optional)

2 small leeks, cleaned, julienned and quickly sautéed until crisp
16 baby carrots, peeled and blanched
8 ounces haricots verts, blanched

THE EUROPEAN INFLUENCE

Green Papaya Salad with Grilled Foie Gras is heavily influenced by the flavors of Europe, since foie gras and basil are both traditionally associated with the continent, as is vinaigrette. Foie gras is known to have been eaten by the Romans, who force-fed their geese and ducks with figs. Nowadays the birds are fed corn.

6 ounces foie gras, cut into 4 slices

¼ cup oyster sauce

½ teaspoon five-spice powder

Mild Chili Cilantro Vinaigrette

1 tablespoon butter

1 teaspoon minced garlic

¾ cup sweet Thai chili sauce

3 tablespoons water

1½ tablespoons chopped cilantro

1½ tablespoons purple basil, finely shredded

Green Papaya Salad

3 cups julienned green papaya

½ cup chopped walnuts

4 sprigs cilantro

16 snow peas, blanched and sliced

16 slices bamboo shoots

1. Marinate the foie gras in the oyster sauce and five-spice powder for at least 30 minutes.

2. Make the vinaigrette. Sauté the garlic in the butter, then, in a bowl, whisk together all the ingredients for the vinaigrette until blended.

3. Toss the green papaya with the walnuts and cilantro.

4. To assemble, place the snow peas and bamboo shoots at the top of each of four plates. Place a mound of the green papaya salad in the center of each plate.

5. Broil or grill the foie gras for about 30 seconds on each side. Place a slice of foie gras on each mound of papaya salad.

6. Drizzle the vinaigrette around the foie gras and serve at once.

Serves 4

Chef Suki at Masons

Green Papaya Salad
with Grilled Foie Gras

Masons, situated on the lowest floor of the vast Fairmont Hotel, on Nob Hill in San Francisco, presents global fusion cuisine. It is an upmarket restaurant with upmarket clientele, and a staff who similarly demand very high standards of one another. This is a perfect reflection of the exacting standards exercised by the executive chef, Chef Suki. His precision and the way he balances food and flavors are a wonder to behold.

Having worked all over the world after leaving Japan, Chef Suki has come to rest, for the moment at least, in an ideal setting for his cross-cultural food. The diners are appreciative and understanding, and he knows that he must provide what his customers desire.

Chef Suki's food is a wonderful combination of ingredients and flavors from all over the world. You can find Chinese and Italian on one plate, Caribbean and Indochinese on another.

Masons

Chef Suki is fascinating to talk to. His ideas have evolved through his constant pre-occupation with food, what he describes as "my journey of food" and his personal challenge to learn more about it – its history, its flavors and its evolution.

Shrimp and Crab Ravioli

1. Sauté the vegetables in the clarified butter until softened.

2. Combine the shrimp and crab with the sherry, cream, soy sauce and sesame oil and season with salt and pepper to taste.

3. With your hands, shape the mixture into four little cakes and sauté in the melted butter until golden brown on both sides.

4. To make the sauce, simmer the shallots in the white wine with the bay leaf until reduced by half. Add the clam juice and cream and simmer until reduced by about two-thirds. Season the sauce with salt and pepper to taste and finish with the truffle butter.

5. Cut two sheets of pasta into four 3-inch squares and the other sheets into four 4-inch squares. Cook the pasta in boiling water for 30 seconds. Drain and pat dry.

6. To assemble the ravioli, place a spoonful of the sautéed vegetables onto each of the smaller pasta squares. Place a seafood cake on top and cover with more vegetables, leaving a thin strip around the edge free of filling. Spoon a little of the sauce over the vegetables and cover each one with a large pasta square.

7. Seal the edges carefully with your fingers.

8. Serve one ravioli on each of four plates and spoon over some of the remaining sauce. Garnish with the sesame seeds and a sprig of chervil.

Serves 4

Chef Suki at Masons

4 large sheets fresh pasta

Vegetables
8 ounces bok choy, finely shredded
6 ounces snow peas, thinly sliced
6 ounces shiitake mushrooms, thinly sliced
2 tablespoons clarified butter

Shrimp and Crab Mixture
6 ounces chopped raw shrimp
4 ounces cooked crabmeat
2 tablespoons medium-dry sherry
2 tablespoons heavy cream
1 tablespoon soy sauce
½ teaspoon sesame oil
¼ cup butter, melted
salt and pepper, to taste

Cream Sauce
2 small shallots, finely chopped
1¼ cups dry white wine
1 small bay leaf
¾ cup bottled clam juice
⅔ cup heavy cream
salt and pepper, to taste
1 tablespoon white truffle butter

Garnish
1 tablespoon black sesame seeds
4 sprigs chervil

2 ducklings, 4–5 pounds each

hickory chips

grilled green onions, to garnish

Marinade

½ cup grated onion

2 tablespoons grated ginger root

2 tablespoons chopped garlic

¾ teaspoon ground cumin

1½ tablespooons tamarind pulp

1½ tablespoons ground turmeric

¾ cup vegetable oil

2 tablespoons soy sauce

1 stalk lemongrass, chopped

2 tablespoons lemon juice

1½ tablespoons shrimp paste

1½ tablespoons chopped Thai basil

Passion Fruit–Grain Mustard Sauce

½ cup sugar

6 tablespoons red wine vinegar

¼ cup passion fruit juice

¼ cup veal stock

2 tablespoons grainy Pommery mustard

½ teaspoon lemon juice

1 teaspoon butter

salt and pepper, to taste

Coconut Banana Fritters

4 bananas, peeled

⅔ cup all-purpose flour

2 eggs, beaten with 2 tablespoons water

½ cup panko (Japanese bread crumbs)
    mixed with ¾ cup grated dried coconut

vegetable oil, for frying

Vegetables

12 baby carrots, peeled and blanched

20 haricots verts, blanched

Roasted Duck
with Coconut Banana Fritter

1. Blanch the ducklings in boiling water to remove some of the fat. Allow to drain and pat dry with paper towels.

2. Combine all the marinade ingredients in a large bowl and marinate the ducklings overnight. Drain well, pat dry and smoke them over the hickory chips. Roast the ducklings to the desired doneness (recommended as medium-rare).

3. Meanwhile, make the sauce. Caramelize the sugar in a large heavy saucepan and add the vinegar. Add the passion fruit juice and stock and simmer until reduced by three-quarters. Add the mustard and lemon juice and finish with the butter. Season with salt and pepper

4. Dust the bananas with the flour, then dip them in the beaten eggs and roll in the panko and coconut mixture. Heat the oil in a deep frying pan to 350–375°F, or until a cube of bread browns in 30 seconds. Deep-fry the bananas until golden.

5. Remove the ducklings from the smoker and allow to rest for about 10 minutes. Cut the ducklings in half and separate each half into a breast, leg and thigh portion.

6. To serve, place half a duckling on each plate, accompany with a fritter, passion fruit sauce and the vegetables. Garnish with the spring onions.

Serves 4

Chef Suki at Masons

"When I'm putting together a dish I'll say, 'well, if I want to have more of an Asian slant to it and one dish has lemon in it, then maybe I'll try lemongrass.' So I think it's interesting and you can go all the way down the line even with white sugar. What is available in other countries to use as sweetening? Well, Thais use a lot of palm sugar and the Chinese use whatever is available there to make their sugar."

Kirk Webber, chef at Cafe Kati

Butterscotch Pudding
with Ginger Whipped Cream

1. Combine the milk, light cream, vanilla and salt in a saucepan, and bring just to a boil to scald. Remove from the heat and reserve.

2. Melt the butter with the brown sugar in a heavy saucepan and cook over low heat until dark caramel, stirring frequently (the longer you cook it the more butterscotch flavor you will get, but do be careful not to let it burn).

3. Gradually add the dark butterscotch mixture to the milk mixture, stirring continually.

4. Blend the cornstarch with the measured water, then whisk into the butterscotch-milk mixture. Return the pan to medium-high heat and continue cooking until thickened, stirring regularly.

5. Lightly beat the egg yolks in a large bowl. Gradually add small amounts of the hot butterscotch mixture to the egg yolks, while whisking all the time. Now pour the pudding mixture into six ¾-cup dishes. To prevent a crust from forming on the top, put some plastic wrap directly on to the pudding surface. Refrigerate for at least 1 hour.

6. Whip the heavy cream until stiff peaks form and then fold in the crystallized ginger. Place a dollop of the whipped cream on top of each pudding just before you serve it and then garnish with a tower of spun sugar, if you wish.

Serves 6

Kirk Webber at Cafe Kati

2½ cups milk

1 cup light cream

1 teaspoon vanilla extract

pinch salt

6 tablespoons butter

1½ cups brown sugar

⅓ cup cornstarch

¼ cup water

3 egg yolks

½ cup heavy cream

3 tablespoons chopped crystallized ginger

tower of spun sugar, to garnish (optional)

SPUN SUGAR

Spun sugar is a wonderfully dramatic garnish to finish this dish off. To make your own tower of spun sugar, pour the desired quantity of plain sugar across a heavy saucepan and cook over a moderate heat until the sugar is melted. Boil until just brown and then quickly dip the pan in cold water to stop it cooking any more. Allow to stand for about 1 minute to thicken. Dip a trimmed whisk (made by cutting the wires of a whisk so that only 2 inches remain attached to the handle) or two forks into the melted sugar and then quickly move back and forth over a suspended rolling pin so that threads of sugar are formed. Continue until all the sugar is used up. Gently lift the spun sugar from the rolling pin and loosely wrap into a circle. The threads of sugar easily become sticky, so try to handle them as little as possible.

1. Lay the pieces of pineapple on a tray and sprinkle with half of the palm sugar to marinate, cover with plastic wrap and leave for 1 hour.
2. Meanwhile place all the remaining ingredients, except the remaining palm sugar, into a blender and purée for 2 minutes, then add the palm sugar and blend for a further 20 seconds.
3. Transfer the purée to an ice cream maker. Freeze according to the manufacturer's instructions. Once the mixture is solid, transfer to a container and place in the freezer.
4. Preheat the broiler to very hot. Lay the marinated pineapple on a foil-lined baking sheet and broil on all sides until it begins to caramelize. (Or grill over a charcoal fire.) Transfer to a plate and cool. Reserve any juices that may have come out in the marinade and pour over the pineapple.
5. To serve, simply place a wedge of the pineapple on a plate and add a scoop of the sorbet.
Serves 6

Peter Gordon at The Sugar Club

1 small pineapple, cut into 6 wedges, core
 and skin removed
1 cup finely grated palm sugar
2 mangoes, peeled and pitted
3 tablespoons finely grated ginger root
1 kaffir lime leaf, stem removed
1 red chili pepper, seeded
7 tablespoons lime juice
¼ cup clear honey

"I am prepared to think sweet, savory and sour can be one dish."

Peter Gordon, chef at The Sugar Club

Grilled Pineapple
with Mango, Ginger and Chili Sorbet

"This, to me, brings Fijian pineapple and Thai mango together in a dessert that would be at home in a Western restaurant."

Chocolate and Pistachio
Steamed Pudding

1. Make the ice cream. Bring the milk, cream and nuts to a boil. Blend the egg yolks with the sugar in a bowl, stir in the milk mixture, return to the pan and cook, stirring continually until thick. Remove from the heat and allow to cool, stirring to prevent a skin forming. Pour into an ice cream maker and freeze according to the manufacturer's instructions.

2. Meanwhile, make the chocolate pudding. Cream the butter with the sugar until light and fluffy. Add the eggs gradually, stirring well with each addition. Stir in the cooled melted chocolate, together with the flour, baking powder and milk. Stir until well blended. Spoon or pipe the mixture into six individual dariole molds so they are just three-quarters full.

3. Cover the molds with foil and steam over gently simmering water for about 40 minutes, until set.

4. Meanwhile, make the pistachio ganache. Bring the milk to a boil in a small saucepan. Add the chocolate and remove from the heat. Stir together until the chocolate has melted completely. Stir in the pistachio nuts. Transfer to a shallow bowl and refrigerate until set almost firm. Once the chocolate puddings are cooked, form the ganache into six balls. Push one ball into the middle of each pudding, re-cover the puddings with foil and keep warm.

5. Make the crème anglaise. Bring the milk and pistachio nuts to a boil. Blend the sugar with the egg yolks in a bowl, stir in the milk mixture, return to the pan and cook, stirring continually until thick. Remove from the heat and allow to cool completely.

6. Make the tuile biscuits. Preheat the oven to 350°F. In a bowl, sift the confectioners' sugar with the flour. Add the egg white, then the melted butter and stir to blend together until smooth. Drop six large spoonfuls of the mixture onto a greased baking sheet and spread out slightly to form six biscuits, leaving at least a 1½-inch space between them, as they will spread. Bake until golden, about 10 minutes. Remove from the oven. Working quickly, take the biscuits from the baking sheet and curl over a rolling pin while still warm and soft. If you want to make the tuile shape as in the photograph, now is the time to do it!

7. To serve, spoon a little crème anglaise onto each of six dessert plates. Unmold a chocolate pudding onto each plate. Put a tuile biscuit on top and drop a scoop of ice cream into the curl of the biscuit.

Serves 6

Chris Benians and Cass Titcombe at The Collection

Pistachio Ice Cream

1 cup milk

⅔ cup heavy cream

¾ cup salted pistachio nuts

6 egg yolks

½ cup sugar

Chocolate Pudding

⅔ cup softened butter

⅔ cup dark brown sugar

2 eggs

2 ounces bitter chocolate, melted and cooled

⅔ cup all-purpose flour

½ teaspoon baking powder

2 tablespoons milk

Pistachio Ganache

2 tablespoons milk

3½ ounces white chocolate

1 tablespoon finely chopped pistachio nuts

Crème Anglaise

¾ cup plus 2 tablespoons milk

¼ cup salted pistachio nuts

¼ cup sugar

4 egg yolks

Tuile Biscuits

½ cup confectioners' sugar

⅓ cup all-purpose flour

¼ cup egg white (about 1 extra-large egg)

3 tablespoons butter, melted

the wok importance

The wok is by far the most widely used utensil in Asia.

It is the piece of cooking equipment that Asian cooks could not be without. Shaped with gently sloping sides and a large usable surface area, the wok is most commonly used for stir-frying. It can also be used for steaming, braising, deep-frying and shallow-frying. It is important that a wok is very hot before adding any oil and that once its protective surface has been scoured away at the beginning of its use, it is never scoured again. After this initial scouring, wipe the wok with paper towels dipped in peanut oil. This is now a seasoned wok. A seasoned wok has a surface that prevents the food from sticking or discoloring, or from picking up any taste from the metal surface.

A wok is fun and practical to use. It gives the opportunity to add large quantities of food because of its size, and the chance to retain control of how the food is cooking: the cook can choose whereabouts in the wok he or she wishes to place the food, thus controlling the amount of heat the food has. Some cooks prefer to wipe or brush the wok with peanut oil after each use. Heavily used woks have a very dark, shiny surface.

There are a number of cooking utensils that go with the wok: a lid, steamer baskets, a shovel or spatula, a slotted spoon and a bamboo brush are the most widely used.

Different cooks have different attitudes to woks. Some use it only for stir-frying, some see it as a large frying pan and some as an intricate utensil. Whatever it is, it is an amazing and versatile piece of equipment.

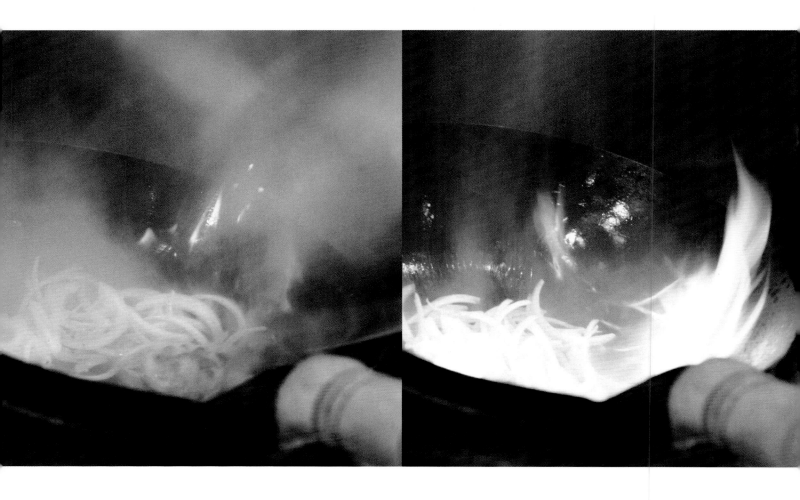

"It's cheap and easy, and it comes up to the heat quite quickly...To cook something decent in a wok you need it to be really hot."

Cass Titcombe, chef at The Collection

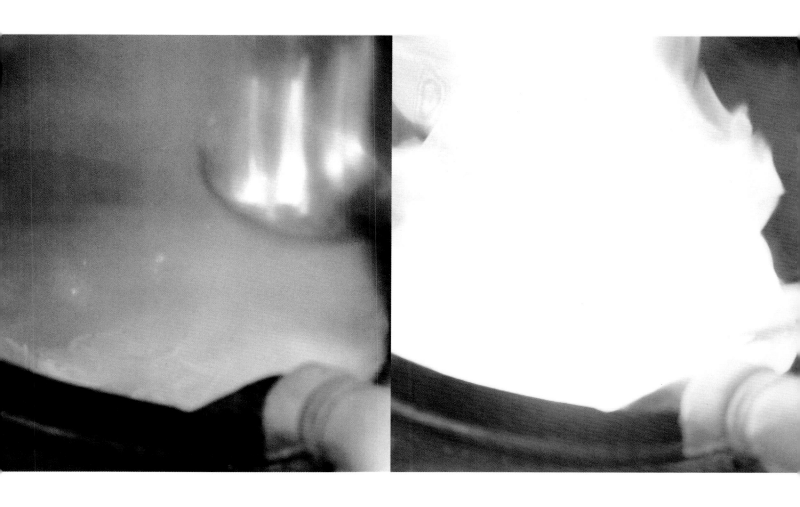

"You can still do it in a frying pan; it's not quite the same but it's not some amazing new technique of cookery, is it? It's a sloping frying pan."

Chris Benians, chef at The Collection

Caramelized Shrimp

Tom Rim

"The wonderful wok! It is easy to use, quick to heat and produces healthier food if it is used properly. Its usefulness is not limited to stir-fries, either. I have braised meat in mine, heated soups, simmered vegetables and smoked lamb. In fact, you could probably add it to my list of utensils that I wouldn't be without."

Michael Lee-Richards, chef at Michael's

2 teaspoons light vegetable oil

2 teaspoons finely chopped garlic

½ small onion, sliced

15 large shrimp, peeled

½ teaspoon ground pepper

1–2 teaspoons chili oil

3 green onions, cut into 1-inch pieces

lettuce leaves, for serving (optional)

Caramel Sauce

½ cup brown sugar

¼ cup fish sauce

½ cup water

1. Start by preparing the caramel sauce. In a small saucepan, combine all the sauce ingredients together and bring to a boil. Continue boiling until the sugar is totally dissolved.

2. Heat the vegetable oil in a wok or large, deep frying pan over high heat, until just smoking. Add the garlic and onion and stir-fry until golden.

3. Add the shrimp, pepper, 2 tablespoons of the caramel sauce and the chili oil and cook until the sauce is thick enough to coat the shrimps, about 2 minutes. Reserve any remaining caramel sauce for later use.

4. Add the green onions and stir-fry the whole thing for about 30 seconds longer. Serve at once, on a bed of lettuce, if desired.

Serves 3

Charles Phan at The Slanted Door

"In the nicest and trendiest restaurants in Hong Kong, you are spending hundreds and hundreds of dollars per person and ninety percent of the items that are coming out on your plate are done in the wok."

Kirk Webber, chef at Cafe Kati

"I am intrigued and driven by flavors that kind of jump in your mouth and sparkle on your tongue and I find a lot of the Vietnamese, Thai, Malaysian and Southeast Asian flavors do that."

Kirk Webber, chef at Cafe Kati

The Slanted Door

This wonderful Vietnamese restaurant, with its cool and stylish high-ceilinged interior, has just a hint of Western influence. The chefs are Asian, while the wait and bar staff are not. The style and approach of the restaurant beautifully complement the Vietnamese menu. The chef, Charles Phan, makes changes to typically Vietnamese dishes where necessary, to accommodate available ingredients and customer demand. He serves a Vietnamese spring roll with the traditional shrimp, pork and mint leaf filling and also a vegetarian version, which uses cabbage, tofu and celery.

Charles Phan's Western influences come from his elimination of much of the fat that is traditionally used in Vietnamese cooking. And as he says, "I change dishes based on what ingredients are available locally. Where if I can find a sea bass, for instance, that can be used for a traditional steamed fish recipe. In Vietnam they use a carp or striped bass, a smaller fish, with the bones and head, the whole thing. You get a lot of flavor with the whole fish. The textures are very different. The fish is very different. I can get sea bass here and most of our clients prefer no bones. But also, it just happens, that sea bass tastes very rich so it is perfect for the dish, so it's a little different. You might not find the exact same dish in Vietnam. The idea is the same."

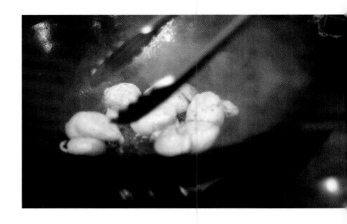

"This dish is a fairly typical Asian one with Asian ingredients, but it does bring a simple and delicious dish into a Western kitchen."

Wok-fried Scallops
with Peanuts, Chili, Bok Choy and Coconut Milk

12 scallops, preferably with the roe intact

¼ cup sesame oil

8 baby bok choy, washed but not dried (the water clinging on to them helps them cook in the wok) and halved lengthwise

1 garlic clove, finely chopped

2 tablespoons finely grated ginger root

1 red chili pepper, cut into rings with the seeds still intact

⅔ cup roasted peanuts, roughly chopped

2 tablespoons grated palm sugar

1 cup canned coconut milk

tamari soy sauce, for seasoning

1. Lightly brush the scallops with some of the oil. Heat up a wok until it begins to smoke and add the scallops, searing them for 10 seconds on each side. Transfer them to a warm plate.

2. Add half the remaining oil to the hot wok, swirling it around for a few seconds. Add the bok choy, which will let off a bit of steam, and toss it every few seconds, browning it a little. Transfer this to a warm plate.

3. Add the remaining oil and once hot, add the garlic, ginger and chili pepper and stir well until they just begin to color. Now toss in the peanuts and sugar and fry for 10 seconds, stirring well to prevent them from burning.

4. Add the coconut milk and bring to a boil, then add the scallops and lay the bok choy on top of them. Cook at a gentle boil for 1 minute, then carefully mix the ingredients together, season with the soy sauce and serve immediately.

Serves 4 as a starter

Peter Gordon at The Sugar Club

BOK CHOY

Bok choy is a Chinese vegetable and is a member of the cabbage family. It has a long white ribbed stalk and green leaves. The leaves can be tough and so are best trimmed. Bok choy needs to be carefully washed too, to be sure all the sand and grit hidden among the leaves are washed away. It tastes best either stir-fried or steamed but, like all cabbages, bok choy can also be boiled.

Bok choy is known by many different names in the various countries of Asia: bai cai, pau tasi, ching tsai, phakket bai and others.

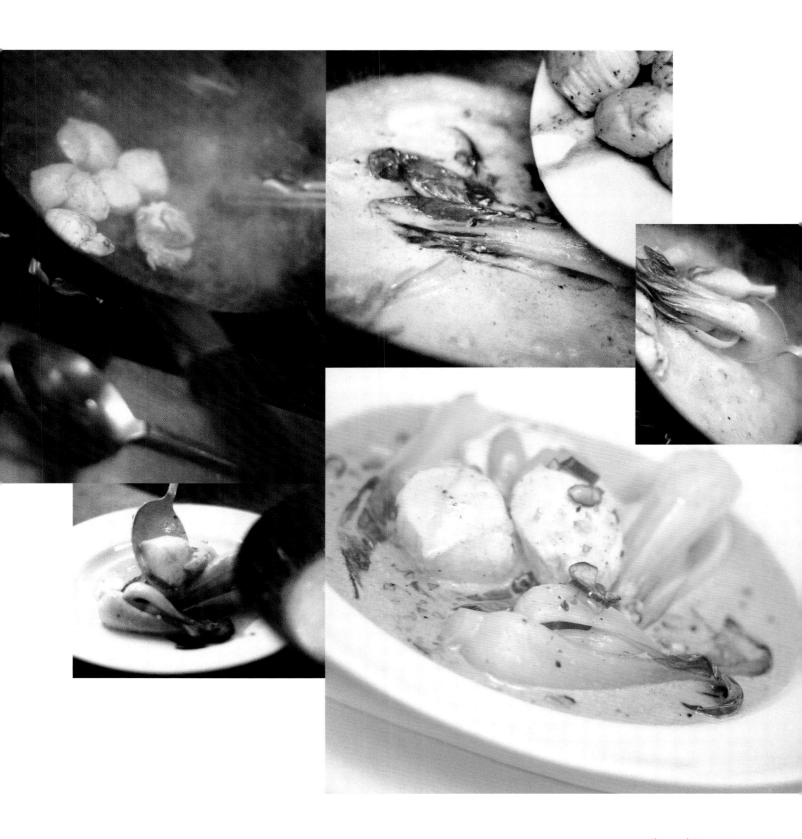

"It's a very difficult piece of equipment. It's so temperamental. Using extremely high heat, you can boil water in 30 seconds. Split-second timing will alter the dish completely. The way you cook in a wok, you are layering the flavors. You add one ingredient, maybe some sort of seasoning, build on that to bring out the maximum flavoring, then the next ingredient, and then the same thing till you finish layering...The guy in the kitchen here is very fast. Not everybody could do that."

Barney Brown, chef at Betelnut

Crab Omelet

1. Whisk 3 eggs in a bowl, add a pinch of salt and a quarter of the mixed herbs and mix well.

2. Heat ½ tablespoon of the oil in a wok, making sure that all of the wok surface is oiled, now pour in the egg mixture and cook the omelet to a nice color. Remove from the wok.

3. Spread 1 tablespoon hoisin sauce thinly over the omelet, add one-quarter of the crabmeat and fold the omelet in half. Serve with a mixed salad. Repeat the process three more times to make four crab omelets.

Serves 4

Graham Harris at Cicada

12 eggs

1 teaspoon salt

7 ounces mixed herbs, chopped

2 tablespoons vegetable oil

¼ cup hoisin sauce

7 ounces cooked crabmeat

mixed salad leaves, to serve

"The wok can be used in so many other ways than just stir-frying, for instance, steaming, deep-frying, poaching, boiling and making omelets. You can easily vary the number of people this omelet can serve: the basis is three eggs per person, and I suggest that you make each omelet separately."

"We, at the restaurant, decided on this name because of the fantastic explosion of flavors. One can almost feel the prawns pop as you eat these wonderful, succulent morsels of the sea."

Volcano Prawns

2 cups light flavorless oil

2 pounds large prawns, deveined

3½ ounces lotus root, sliced

6 asparagus spears

2 tablespoons Chinese cooking wine

2 cups cilantro leaves, julienned, to garnish

Volcano Prawn Sauce

1 tablespoon chili sauce

1 tablespoon fermented white bean curd

¾ cup plus 2 tablespoons tomato paste
  (or 1 cup tomato juice)

1 tablespoon finely chopped lemongrass

3 tablespoons finely chopped red Hungarian
  chili peppers

½ teaspoon grated mandarin zest

1. In a wok, heat the oil until very hot. Add the prawns and toss in the hot oil until nearly cooked through. Add the lotus root and asparagus spears and cook for a further minute.

2. Remove the prawns and vegetables with a slotted spoon. Drain off the oil. Rinse the wok in hot water.

3. Combine all the sauce ingredients together and heat through over a moderate heat for 10 minutes.

4. Return the prawns and the vegetables to the wok, then add the Chinese cooking wine and ¾ cup plus 2 tablespoons of the sauce (or more for a spicier taste). Continue to toss the prawns until the sauce coats them very well.

5. Transfer the prawns to a plate and serve garnished with a julienne of cilantro.

Serves 4

Stanislaus Soares at Chinois

> "Yet another use for the multipurpose wok! Be very careful not to overfill the wok and not to get the oil too hot, as this will burn the fish before it is cooked. This is a recipe that will take some time, but it will be well worth it."

Deep-fried Whole Fish

four 11-ounce whole fish, cleaned, gutted and sliced through to the bone on both sides, but not through the bone. Suitable fish to use are bream, bass, snapper, mackerel and pomfret.

oil for deep-frying

banana leaf squares, cut to size (optional)

Dressing

2 garlic cloves

4 cilantro roots

2 green chili peppers, chopped

¼ cup lime juice

1 tablespoon fish sauce

Garnish

oil for deep-frying

8 garlic cloves, thinly sliced

1 large shallot, cut in half lengthwise and thinly sliced

3 red chilies, thinly sliced at an angle

3½ ounces mixed herbs (Thai basil, cilantro, mint, Chinese chives)

2 limes, halved

1. Start by making the dressing. Pound the garlic, cilantro roots and chilies together using a pestle and mortar. Add all the remaining dressing ingredients and adjust the seasoning as necessary.

2. Next prepare the garnish. In a wok, heat the oil to 350–375°F, or until a cube of bread browns in 30 seconds. Add the garlic slices and fry until golden, then remove and drain. Add the shallot and fry until golden. Remove and drain. Finally, add the chilies and fry them until golden; remove and drain.

3. To cook the fish, heat some more oil in the wok oil to 350–375°F, or until a cube of bread browns in 30 seconds. Add the fish, fry until cooked and crispy, then remove and drain off the excess oil. Place each fish on a banana leaf, if you like. Pour over some dressing and garnish with the herbs, half a lime and the deep-fried garnish.

Serves 4

Graham Harris at Cicada

the noodle knack

Noodles have been in existence since the 1st century BC

They came about because of the advent of grain mills, and it is probably the Chinese who should be credited for their invention, although there is something of a question mark over that.

Noodles exist in all sorts of guises: brown or white, flat, thin or square, rice noodles and glass noodles, just to scratch the surface. The varying flavors and textures are the result of different starch bases. Whatever form they take, noodles are a food that is enjoyed throughout the world.

Many people view noodles as Asia's pasta. This may or may not be an accurate representation of them, but it does clarify one point: for a lot of us, noodles are easy and accessible in a way that is similar to pasta. And they are made from the same ingredients as pasta: flour, egg and water, and sometimes just flour and water.

Because of their infinite variety of shapes and sizes, noodles can be both a light accompaniment or a more substantial provider. They carry sauces and dressings well, enhance a soup, amply accompany any fish, meat or vegetables, and are delicious on their own with just the barest of additions, to make a complete meal. It is because of their diversity that noodles go so well with East-West food. They sit well in either type of food, or happily in the middle.

For Asians, noodles are a part of the most basic of their diets. When you see or hear a Japanese person slurping down their noodles, that is exactly what they are supposed to do. It demonstrates their enthusiasm for, and approval of, the food.

Noodles can be bought both fresh and dry. Dry noodles store well for up to a year in a cool, dark place, whereas fresh, which are always preferable, keep in the refrigerator for two or three days.

"Noodles are easy to make, cheap, and easy to transport."

Kirk Webber, chef at Cafe Kati

"The latest thing now is Asian noodles. It's fast, it's healthy. You'll see them everywhere, noodle shops opening up left and right."

Barney Brown, chef at Betelnut

"These fresh spring rolls are simply a Vietnamese salad wrapped in rice paper. It can be difficult to learn how to roll the rice wrapper around all the filling tightly. It helps if the water used to dip the rice paper wrap is approximately 110°F; otherwise, they become brittle and break easily. If you are in a hurry, simply julienne the filling ingredients and roll the paper around them."

Fresh Mango Spring Rolls

1. Soak the vermicelli in the measured water for about 15 minutes. Drain and set aside.

2. To assemble the spring rolls, dip a sheet of rice paper in water (approximately 110°F and transfer to a work surface that is covered with a damp tea towel. After about 30 seconds, or when it is pliable, place a lettuce leaf over the bottom two-thirds of the rice paper, leaving a 1-inch border of paper at the bottom.

3. Place 2 tablespoons of vermicelli, 1 tablespoon of grated carrot, 2 slices of mango, some bean sprouts, basil and mint on top of the lettuce leaf. Fold up the bottom 1-inch border of rice paper and place over the filling. Fold upward again to enclose the filling. Fold in the right, then the left edges of the rice paper. Continue folding until a tight cylinder is formed. Transfer to a serving platter and cover with damp paper towels until ready to serve. Repeat to make 8 rolls.

4. Just before serving, cut the spring rolls in half and accompany with the vinaigrette as a dipping sauce.

Makes 8

Kirk Webber at Cafe Kati

2 ounces thin rice vermicelli

2 cups warm water

eight 8-inch round rice papers

4 large lettuce leaves, ribs removed and
   leaves halved lengthwise

1 large carrot, grated

2 mangoes, peeled and thinly sliced

4 ounces bean sprouts

½ cup basil leaves

½ cup mint leaves

1 quantity Spicy Thai Vinaigrette
   (see page 180)

As it says on the door, Cafe Kati is a blend of East and West cuisine. Set to the west of Japantown and south of Pacific Heights in San Francisco, this is a restaurant that has grown out of the vision of chef Kirk Webber and his wife, Tina. Although the neighborhood was rough when the restaurant first opened seven years ago, it is slowly getting easier, and they have had a lot of good press, which obviously encourages clientele. They have now settled into the neighborhood.

The restaurant appears small, divided into two rooms. There is a narrow passage between the two, which also takes you past the open kitchen. It has a relaxed atmosphere and attentive wait staff. The food looks fantastic and tastes delicious. Kirk Webber is heavily influenced by the opportunity of Asian ingredients, and he uses his knowledge of them together with his contacts within the industry, which he has built up. He uses the best ingredients available.

Cafe Kati

As a chef, Kirk is aware how visual his food is, and makes the distinction between how men and women react to it, but suggests that "everything is based on strong flavors and if it looks good it still tastes good."

Thai Coconut Broth

1. Bring the measured water to a boil and add the coconut, coconut milk and cream. Turn the heat down to low and let the mixture simmer for 5 minutes. Then put in a blender and purée on high speed for about 5 minutes. Strain through a fine sieve.

2. Place the lemongrass, celery, carrots and onion in a stainless steel pan together with the lime leaves (if using) and juice, fish sauce, peppercorns and clam juice.

3. Bring to a boil, cover and let simmer for 20 minutes. Strain the mixture through a fine sieve and add to the coconut cream.

4. Add the ginger, garlic, chili and beet garnish while still hot. Adjust the seasoning with salt and white pepper.

Serving ideas: cover some seafood of your choice with the Thai broth and poach (do not boil) until just cooked. Serve over crispy rice noodles. Top with a chiffonade of Thai basil, cilantro sprigs and sliced green onions. You can also add a fine julienne of wood ear mushrooms to the broth, and you could wrap some of the garnish in a strip of cucumber.

Serves 4

Kirk Webber at Cafe Kati

SLICING INTO A CHIFFONADE

Any leaf vegetable or herb can be sliced into a chiffonade. Stack the leaves and roll them tightly, then slice down the length of the roll at very small intervals to achieve thin strips.

1 cup water

1½ cups unsweetened dried coconut

1¾ cups canned coconut milk

¼ cup heavy cream

2 stalks lemongrass, thinly sliced

2 stalks celery, thinly sliced

2 small carrots, peeled and thinly sliced

1 onion, thinly sliced

6 kaffir lime leaves (optional)

2 tablespoons lime juice

3 tablespoons fish sauce, or to taste

1 tablespoon whole black peppercorns

3 cups bottled clam juice

salt and white pepper, to taste

Garnish

1 knob ginger root, peeled and thinly sliced

4 medium to large garlic cloves, thinly sliced

1–2 serrano chili peppers, thinly sliced

one 2-ounce yellow beet, julienned

"This recipe in many ways is a pick-and-mix from many cuisines, notably Japan and Spain – two of my favorites."

Soba, Tuna, Piquillo Pepper
and Wild Asparagus Salad

1. In a bowl, mix the tuna with the lime juice and the ginger. Place in the refrigerator, covered, and leave to marinate for 1 hour.

2. Next cook the soba noodles by bringing a large pot of water to a boil. Add the salt and carefully add the soba noodles, stir gently. Once the pot comes back to a boil add 1¼ cups of the measured cold water and bring back to a boil again. Add the remaining 1¼ cups of measured cold water and again return it to a boil. Test a noodle; it should now be done, but still slightly firm. Drain in a colander and then refresh with cold water. Drain and mix gently with the sesame oil and set aside.

3. Once the tuna has been marinating for its hour, stir in the tamari soy sauce, then add all the remaining ingredients, mix everything together gently and serve.

Serves 4 as a starter

Peter Gordon at The Sugar Club

10 ounces tuna fillet, cut into ½-inch dice

2 tablespoons lime juice

2 tablespoons finely grated ginger root

7 ounces soba noodles (use ones that are 35–40 percent buckwheat flour)

1 teaspoon salt

2½ cups water

1½ tablespoons sesame oil

1 teaspoon tamari soy sauce

4 piquillo or other hot chili peppers, cut into ¼-inch-wide strips

5 ounces wild asparagus, blanched and refreshed

1½ tablespoons extra-virgin olive oil

1⅓ cups finely sliced green onions

SOBA NOODLES

Soba noodles are a principal Japanese noodle found frequently in soup and cold salads. They are mostly made from buckwheat flour and are available fresh, dried or precooked. Their appearance is thin, flat and grayish brown. Soba noodles are incredibly nutritious, containing fiber, protein, vitamins, rutin, calcium and iron.

The critics "don't realize there's as much skill required...and in many ways more if you bring disparate ingredients together. If you bring in something from another place, you have got to know how it's going to work, and in what proportion, and how to do it and why they work. That's the tricky bit, so I think there's a real knowledge behind it."

Peter Gordon, chef at The Sugar Club

Seafood Claypot

1. Heat the oil in a large stockpot, add the curry powder and stir for 1 minute or until fragrant.

2. Add the stock, sugar, lemongrass, lime leaves, chili peppers (if using), and fish sauce. Bring to a boil, lower the heat and simmer for 20 minutes.

3. Add the glass noodles and cook for 1 minute.

4. Add the seafood together with the corn and mushrooms, cover the pot and cook for about 4 minutes or just until the shellfish is open and the fish is firm to the touch.

5. Divide the seafood mixture among four large soup bowls or six smaller bowls. Pour over the soup, top with green onions and serve hot.

Serves 4–6

Barney Brown at Betelnut

STRAW MUSHROOMS

Straw mushrooms are available canned in brine. They are one of Asia's most important mushrooms. They are commonly grown on paddy straw, hence their name, but they also grow on dried stems or leaves. Their appearance is like two mushrooms end to end and, in fact, their Chinese name means double mushroom. Straw mushrooms are small, a grayish-brown and have a pale stem.

1 tablespoon vegetable oil

2 tablespoons curry powder or paste

6 cups fish or chicken stock (canned stock can be substituted)

½ teaspoon sugar

1 stalk fresh lemongrass, sliced

6 kaffir lime leaves (or the zest of 1 lime)

2 teaspoons sliced hot chili peppers (optional)

3 tablespoons fish sauce

4 ounces glass noodles (mung bean threads), soaked in cold water

1 pound mixed fresh seafood (cleaned mussels, clams, shrimp, squid and white fish)

1 cup canned or cooked fresh baby corn

⅔ cup drained, canned straw mushrooms

sliced green onions, to garnish

"The whole idea of Betelnut is based on the beer gardens of Southeast Asia, and we wanted to see what it was like to create something like that, because it seemed such a great idea. The beer gardens there have a lot of spicy, unusual exotic foods together with lots of ice-cold mugs of beer."

Barney Brown, chef at Betelnut

1. Make the broth. Heat the oil in a large stockpot. Add the shallots, garlic, ginger, peanuts, chili peppers, dried shrimp, shrimp paste, lemongrass and curry powder. Cook, stirring, for about 5 minutes.

2. Add the chicken stock, coconut milk, fish sauce and sugar. Bring to a boil, reduce the heat and simmer gently for 20 minutes. The broth can be refrigerated at this point.

3. While the broth is simmering, fry the tofu and shallots separately in the oil until crisp and golden. Set aside.

4. Cook the soaked rice noodles in a pan of boiling water for 1 minute. Drain and divide among four soup bowls. Add the bean sprouts to the rice noodles.

5. Heat 8 cups of the broth to boiling, then add the shrimp and fried tofu. Pour over the bowls of cooked noodles and top with the quail's eggs, fried shallots and laksa leaves.

Serves 4

Barney Brown at Betelnut

Laksa Broth

1 tablespoon vegetable oil

⅓ cup finely chopped shallots

2 tablespoons finely chopped garlic

2 tablespoons finely chopped ginger root

½ cup finely chopped unsalted roasted peanuts

2 tablespoons seeded and finely chopped red chili peppers

2 tablespoons chopped dried shrimp

1 teaspoon shrimp paste

½ stalk lemongrass, finely chopped

2 tablespoons curry powder

6 cups chicken stock

4 cups canned coconut milk

3 tablespoons fish sauce

½ tablespoon sugar

Laksa Lemak

½-inch tofu squares

¼ cup sliced shallots

1 tablespoon vegetable oil

12 ounces rice noodles (banh pho), soaked in cold water

4 ounces bean sprouts

12 large shrimp, heads and shells on

4 quail's eggs, hard boiled, peeled and cut in half

laksa leaves (also known as Vietnamese mint), to garnish

Laksa Lemak

Melon and Ginger
Glass Noodle Soup

1. Peel and seed the melon. Cut the flesh into large chunks and purée until smooth. Refrigerate.

2. Bring the measured water to a boil with half the ginger and sugar. Once the water is boiling, add the noodles and simmer for 5 minutes. Remove from the heat and allow to stand so that the noodles can absorb the liquid. Remove the ginger, then transfer the noodles to a bowl and refrigerate until well chilled.

3. Combine the lime juice with the remaining sugar and ginger in a small saucepan. Bring to a boil, then reduce the heat and simmer until the syrup thickens. Remove from the heat, discard the ginger and allow the mixture to cool.

4. Make the biscuits. Brush the filo pastry with the egg white and sprinkle all over with the confectioners' sugar and cinnamon. Fold width-wise in half and cover with more egg white, confectioners' sugar and cinnamon. Roll the pastry up into a tube starting from a short end, then cut across into six cylindrical biscuits.

5. Melt the butter in a sauté pan. Add the biscuits and fry until golden on both sides. Drain on paper towels.

6. To serve, half fill a very large serving bowl with crushed ice. Set a slightly smaller serving bowl in the ice and pour in the melon purée. Add the glass noodles and ginger lime syrup. Serve the soup accompanied by a cinnamon biscuit.

Serves 6

Chris Benians and Cass Titcombe at The Collection

1 Charentais melon, 1⅔ pound

3 cups water

2 ounces ginger root, peeled and thinly sliced

½ cup sugar

10 ounces glass noodles (mung bean threads)

juice of 2 limes

Cinnamon Biscuits

1 sheet filo pastry

1 egg white

3 tablespoons confectioners' sugar

2 teaspoons ground cinnamon

2 tablespoons butter

Crispy Noodles
with Chicken and Vegetables

1. Heat the oil in a deep-fat fryer until very hot, 350–375°F, or until a cube of bread browns in 30 seconds. Fry the noodles in the oil until crispy and then drain on paper towels. Place them in a bowl and keep warm.

2. In a hot wok, toss the chicken pieces until nearly cooked through. Add the vegetables, including the chili, and continue to stir-fry until the vegetables are just done, by which time the chicken should be cooked. Transfer to a warmed dish.

3. Rinse out the wok, then add the chicken stock, wine, light soy, salt and sugar. Bring to a boil and return the chicken and vegetables to the wok.

4. Finish off by heating through and mixing in the mushroom soy and sesame oil. Pour over the crispy noodles and serve.

Serves 1

Stanislaus Soares at Chinois

7 tablespoons light flavorless oil

7 ounces wheat noodles

5 ounces skinless chicken breast, cut into
   1-inch pieces

2 asparagus spears

1 bok choy

10 sugar snap peas

2 brown mushrooms

1 red Hungarian chili pepper, seeded and
   chopped, or a bird's eye chili for more spice

⅔ cup chicken stock

¼ cup Chinese cooking wine

1 tablespoon light soy sauce

1 teaspoon salt

2 teaspoons sugar

2 tablespoons mushroom soy

1 teaspoon sesame oil

the chili touch

Until you know the strength of a chili,
always proceed with caution.

There are varying degrees of heat that come from a chili, and this variation depends on the size, shape, color and variety. That said, heat can vary from one chili to another coming from the same plant. The heat from chilies comes from the whole vegetable, but the tip is the mildest, and the area where the seeds attach to the membrane the hottest. The best way to proceed, particularly if you are unfamiliar with chilies, is to test: take a small taster from the tip of a fresh chili, or place the tiniest amount of chili powder on a dampened finger.

Chili powder also varies in its strength. This depends from which plant it was made, and whether anything has been added to the powder. Mexican chili powder, for instance, always has cumin added. There are also chili pastes, sauces and oil, all of which vary in heat. A chili oil that is sold in a bottle containing the seeds and whole chilies will gradually get hotter and hotter the longer it is kept.

If you are unfamiliar with the type of chili you are using, add it gradually, taste-testing for hotness as you go. Chilies need not be over-powering: they can hugely enhance a dish and are used constantly in Asian, South American, Californian, Texan and North and West African cooking. Used to the best effect, chilies add exactly the right kick but do not dominate the dish.

There is no one country that grows all the many varieties of chili, and that can be part of the chili experience. Experimentation, knowledge and use lead to "knowing" chilies more, thereby making them greater fun to use, and less of an unknown quantity.

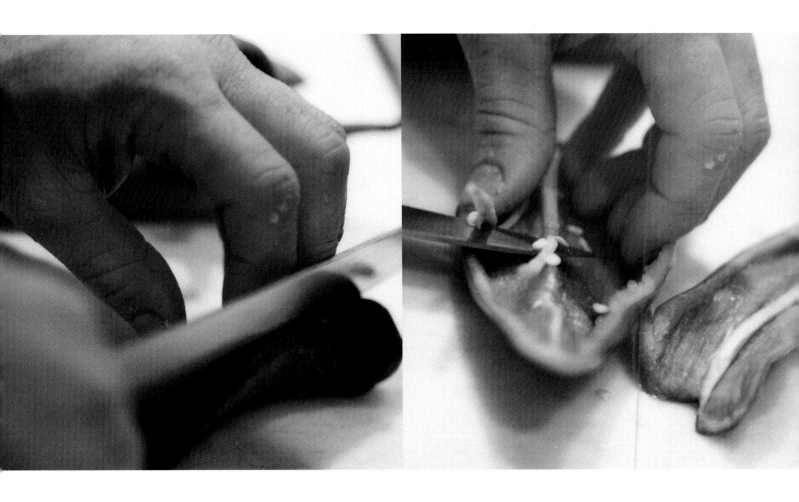

"There are quite a lot of ingredients I would not be without, definitely chilies."

Cass Titcombe, chef at The Collection

"Sometimes changing a menu is a matter of exchanging ingredients. For example, I might have as a main course on my menu a dish of crispy duck with bok choy and smoked chilies, then decide that the smoked chilies would be a perfect starter with home-cured pork. The bok choy could end up wok-fried with scallops, and I might turn the duck into a fritter with lime leaves."

Peter Gordon, chef at The Sugar Club

12 lamb cutlets

salt

2 orange sweet potatoes, peeled and cut into
   1-inch dice

¼ cup sesame oil

2 red chili peppers, finely sliced with the
   seeds intact

3 thumbs ginger root, peeled and julienned

½ cup cilantro leaves

¾ cup plus 2 tablespoons boiling water

pepper

Chili and Mint Salsa

3 mild green chili peppers, seeded, stems
   removed, and finely sliced

1 cup mint leaves, shredded

1 tablespoon fish sauce

2 tablespoons grated palm sugar

1 white onion, finely diced

juice and finely grated zest of 3 limes

3 tablespoons peanut oil

7 ounces sugar snap peas

1. Lightly season the lamb cutlets with salt and leave to sit at room temperature for 1 hour, covered with plastic wrap.

2. Preheat the oven to 400°F. In a bowl, mix the sweet potatoes, sesame oil, red chili peppers and ginger; season with salt and pepper and transfer to a roasting dish. Pour on the measured boiling water, then cook in the oven until just done, about 45 minutes. Once cooked, mix in the cilantro leaves and keep warm.

3. While the sweet potatoes are cooking, make the salsa. Mix the green chili peppers with the mint, fish sauce, sugar, onion, lime juice and zest and the peanut oil and leave to sit for at least 30 minutes.

4. Preheat a broiler or prepare a fire in a grill. Broil or grill the lamb cutlets for about 2 minutes on each side. Blanch the sugar snap peas in boiling water, leaving them still crunchy.

5. Serve the cutlets on top of the sweet potatoes and sugar snaps and drizzle the salsa over the top.

Serves 4 as a main course

Peter Gordon at The Sugar Club

PALM SUGAR

This sweetener comes from the sap of a flowering palm tree. Skilled workers climb up the palm tree, gently beat the inflorescence and then hang a container in which to catch the sap. The sap is boiled down, at which point it becomes heavy and moist, and is evaporated before being poured into cylindrical bamboo containers. Palm sugar is very dense and sticky and is sold either in the cylindrical shapes in which it is made, or in jars or rounded cakes. The surface of the sugar is sometimes sealed with wax.

Grilled Lamb Cutlets

with Green Chili and Mint Salsa on Spicy Roast Sweet Potatoes and Sugar Snaps

"This dish is a remake of lamb and mint sauce, but really fresh and tasty."

Chicken and Char Siu Salad
with Pickled Vegetables

1. Place the chicken breasts in a shallow dish, and pour over the char siu sauce, sesame oil and Japanese seasoning. Cover and marinate in the refrigerator for at least 24 hours.

2. Make the pickled vegetables. In a saucepan, combine the measured water with the rice vinegar, sugar, salt, garlic, chili and ginger root. Bring to a boil, place the cauliflower, carrot and cucumber in a bowl, remove the pan from the heat and pour the mixture over the vegetables. Cover the bowl, allow the mixture to cool completely, then drain the vegetables.

3. Preheat a broiler. Remove the chicken from the marinade and broil on both sides until just cooked through. Allow to cool slightly, then cut across into thin slices.

4. To serve, combine the salad leaves with the pickled vegetables in a large bowl and toss together. Arrange a little of the mixture in the center of each of four plates. Lay some chicken slices on top and cover with more salad. Continue layering, then garnish the top with the cashew nuts.

Serves 4

Chris Benians and Cass Titcombe at The Collection

2 boneless, skinless chicken breasts

3 tablespoons char siu sauce (or teryaki sauce)

1 tablespoon sesame oil

1 teaspoon Japanese seven spices seasoning (shichimi)

Asian salad leaves, for serving

¾ cup roasted salted cashew nuts, coarsely chopped, to garnish

Pickled Vegetables

2 cups water

1 cup rice vinegar

½ cup superfine sugar

1 tablespoon salt

2 garlic cloves, finely chopped

1 chili pepper, seeded and finely chopped

1 small piece ginger root, peeled and finely chopped

1 cup sliced cauliflower florets

1 large carrot, julienned

½ cucumber, seeded and julienned

Betelnut

Betelnut, situated in the upmarket Cow Hollow area of San Francisco, is crafted after the beer gardens found all over Southeast Asia, where you find mugs of ice-cold beer and little plates of a variety of foods. The tables at Betelnut are laid with plates in the center and a pot of chopsticks. One of the key elements of Southeast Asian beer gardens is the idea that the food be shared among everyone at the table. Obviously not all of Betelnut's customers want to participate in the custom of sharing, but as Barney Brown, the chef at Betelnut, says, "It is an educational experience for our customers and for our staff, for everybody." Diners can decide among themselves whether or not they want to share.

For Barney Brown, his food is authentic Southeast Asian and not fusion food. Betelnut is involved in the fusion food phenomenon, however, because their menu offers a selection of dishes from Japan down to Singapore, so if customers make the choice to share, they can mix the dishes as they choose. If they don't, each can choose his or her own dish and on the table will be a feast of foods from all over Southeast Asia.

Sun-dried Anchovies
with Peanuts and Chili Peppers

oil for deep-frying

4 ounces sun-dried anchovies (also known in Southeast Asia as ikan bilis, ikan teri or kung yue)

1 tablespoon chopped garlic

1 tablespoon sliced, seeded hot red and green chili peppers

2½ cups chopped green onions, white part only

1 cup unsalted roasted peanuts

salt and white pepper, to taste

1. Heat the oil in a deep frying pan until hot, 350–375°F, or until a cube of bread browns in 30 seconds. Fry the anchovies for about 1 minute or until crisp. Pat dry on paper towels.

2. Heat a wok or sauté pan, add a little oil, then stir-fry the garlic and chili peppers for about 1 minute or until fragrant. Add the green onions and peanuts and stir-fry for 1–2 minutes longer.

3. Add the anchovies and toss lightly to mix. Season with salt and white pepper. Serve immediately with ice-cold beer.

Serves 4

Barney Brown at Betlenut

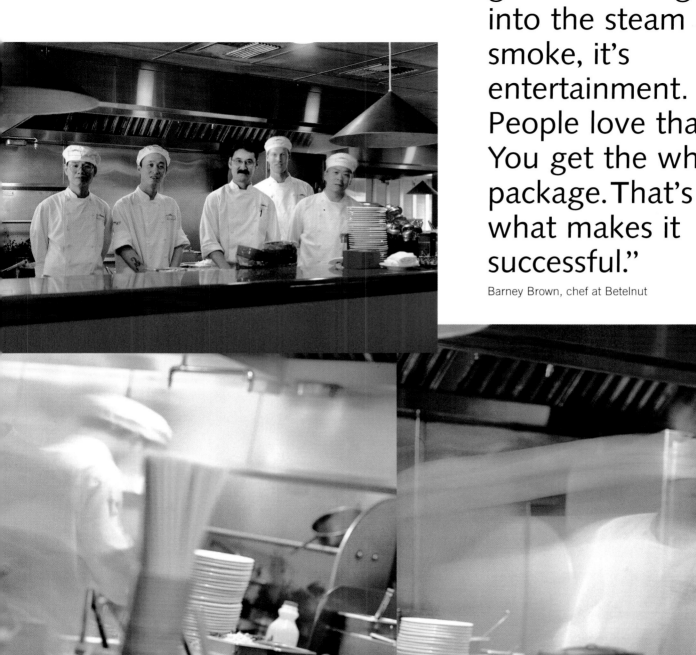

"At Betelnut you get a show, right into the steam and smoke, it's entertainment. People love that. You get the whole package. That's what makes it successful."

Barney Brown, chef at Betelnut

"This is a great side dish to get your friends talking. It's unusual yet tasty, real party-warming food. The chilies are hot, although roasting them takes a little of the heat out, but they are still full of flavor."

Stuffed Chilies

1. Preheat the oven to 350°F. Meanwhile, heat the butter in a small frying pan and sauté the chopped shallot until golden.

2. Roast the red or green chilies in the preheated oven for 10 minutes. Remove and allow to cool.

3. Make a lengthwise slit down one side of each chili. Open up the chilies flat, remove the seeds and set aside. Combine the pork with the green onion, garlic, cilantro, fish sauce, and sautéd shallot and mix well.

4. Stuff the chilies with the pork mixture and then reshape each chili back to its original shape, around the pork. Dust the chilies with flour and then dip in the tempura batter.

5. Heat the oil to 350–375°F, or until a cube of bread browns in 30 seconds. Add the stuffed chilies and fry until golden brown. Remove, drain well and serve.

Serves 4 or 5 as a side dish

Graham Harris at Cicada

1 tablespoon butter

1 shallot, finely diced

12 medium-large red or green chilies
(depending on how brave you are)

4 ounces ground pork

1 green onion, cut into fine rings

1 garlic clove, crushed

2 cups cilantro leaves, chopped

dash of bottled fish sauce, to taste

all-purpose flour for dusting

about 1 cup tempura batter (tempura batter
mix can be found in most Asian stores)

oil for deep-frying

"At the restaurant I use fillets of baby snapper, which are available from Port Phillip Bay. The line-caught fish, of course, being a lot better."

Red Chili Butter
with Steamed Baby Barramundi Fillets

7 tablespoons soft unsalted butter

1 teaspoon finely chopped garlic

½ teaspoon paprika

½ teaspoon ground cumin

1 tablespoon olive oil

2 bird's eye chili peppers, finely chopped

1 tablespoon shredded Asian basil (the leaf is much smaller than normal basil with a very pronounced sweet flavor)

¼ teaspoon salt

¼ teaspoon pepper

1 tablespoon lemon juice

two 6-ounce barramundi (or snapper) fillets

1. In a bowl and a warm place, cream the butter with a wooden spoon to get it very soft.

2. In a small pan, sauté the garlic and spices in the olive oil. Add this to the butter and mix well, then fold in the chopped chili peppers, basil, seasoning and lemon juice.

3. Steam the barramundi fillets for around 4–5 minutes until just done. Top with the red chili butter. This melts very readily on the fish and almost forms a sauce. This is best eaten simply with steamed jasmine rice and steamed bok choy.

Serves 2

Stanislaus Soares at Chinois

"These apricots are a delicious treat. You'll probably have to go shopping for them in a high-quality health food shop, but they're well worth it. They still contain the pit and are totally different in taste from your usual dried apricot. They are rich enough to take on the other flavors in this odd-sounding dish."

Chili-poached Hunza Apricots
with Spice Biscuits and Mascarpone

1. Bring the sugar and measured water gently to a simmer in a deep saucepan, then boil it until it turns a golden brown, making sure you do not stir as it may crystallize.

2. Quickly add the sliced chili peppers and stir for a few seconds, then add both the citrus juices. Be careful as these will start to spit when they touch the hot syrup, so stand well clear.

3. Now add the apricots to the pan and slowly bring the liquid back to a boil, adding enough of the reserved soaking liquid to just cover the fruit. Cover the pan and simmer for 20 minutes. Remove from the heat and leave the apricots to cool in the liquid.

4. Meanwhile make the spice biscuits. Preheat the oven to 325°F.

5. Cream the butter and sugar together until light in color. Sift the flour and cornstarch with the baking powder into the butter mixture. Add the remaining ingredients and mix gently until the dough holds together.

6. Divide the dough into six even-sized pieces. Roll each piece into a long sausage shape and place them on a baking sheet lined with parchment paper, about 3 inches apart. Gently press the biscuits down with a fork dipped in flour.

7. Bake in the oven for 15 minutes. The biscuits shouldn't color too much, so keep an eye on them. Once cooked, remove from the oven and let them cool on the baking sheet for a few minutes before transferring them to a wire rack to cool. Store in an airtight jar.

8. Serve the apricots with mascarpone and a spice biscuit.

Serves 6

Peter Gordon at The Sugar Club

1½ cups unrefined superfine sugar

½ cup water

2 medium-hot red chili peppers, finely sliced with seeds intact

½ cup lemon juice

½ cup orange juice

24 dried Hunza apricots, briefly rinsed, then soaked in cold water for 2 hours and drained, reserving the liquid

mascarpone cheese, to serve

Spice Biscuits

⅔ cup unsalted butter, at room temperature

¼ cup Demerana sugar

⅔ cup all-purpose flour, plus a little for dipping

¾ cup plus 2 tablespoons cornstarch

½ teaspoon baking powder

½ green chili pepper, seeded and finely chopped

½ teaspoon freshly ground cloves

½ teaspoon finely grated lime zest

"The Chocolate Chili Sorbet is a little bit unusual to serve, but it is a curiously interesting sorbet. I love it, but at this stage I must say it's not chili hot to savor! Fresh raspberries make a lovely accompaniment to this sorbet."

Chocolate Chili Sorbet

1¼ cups butter

1⅔ cups cocoa powder (Cocoa Barry preferably)

3 cups sugar

1 tablespoon coffee extract

1 teaspoon Sichuan chili powder

7 cups water

1. Put all the ingredients together in a copper pot and bring to a boil. Reduce the heat and simmer for 20 minutes. Make sure the mixture does not have any lumps at all.

2. Remove from heat and cool completely. Freeze in an ice cream maker according to the manufacturer's instructions. Then transfer to a clean, dry freezer container, cover and keep frozen to use as required.

Serves 6

Stanislaus Soares at Chinois

a taste of rice

When choosing rice, it is important to take into account the grain, aroma, flavor, firmness, stickiness and the feel of it in your mouth.

Rice is the staple ingredient for over half the population of the world. The very poorest of our world population eat only rice. It is the staple of the Asian diet, and with that being the case, it is fundamental and respected. All types of rice are nonfattening, cheap, gluten free, absorbent and easy to cook. There are many schools of thought on how to cook rice, the main difference being whether to boil it or steam it. Steaming is also known as the absorption method. With either method, the rice does absorb water.

Each type of rice absorbs liquid in a different way, and obviously each rice variety differs in flavor. These factors determine the type of meal the rice is best eaten with, and at what stage in the meal it should be served. The huge variety of rice available makes it incredibly versatile: it can be served with virtually any type of food, simply as an accompaniment or as an intrinsic part of the dish.

Polished rice is superior to unpolished rice and the best rice is aged, which means it has been stored for some time. Unpolished rice has a layer of bran. Rice is described or classified sometimes by grain and sometimes by origin, for example long-grain rice and basmati rice. That said, there are three basic categories of rice in the multitude of those available: long-grain, short-grain and long-grain with a tendency to be sticky. Short-grain rice is somewhat softer but not fluffy. It can be clingy. The various types of rice require different cooking techniques, and this can depend upon the dish in which the rice is to be used.

"Rice...people don't perceive that to be starch."

Chris Benians, chef at The Collection

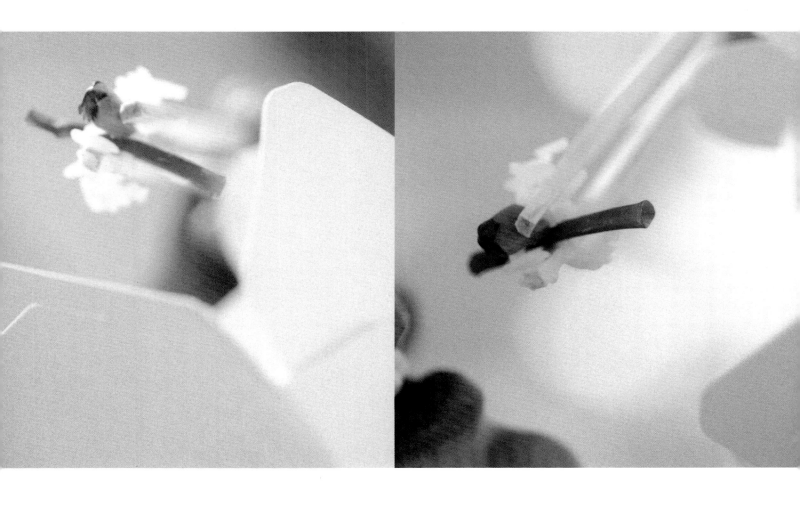

"We have lots of different rices. Japanese rices for when Japanese people come here. I have sushi on the menu tomorrow, so I have to use Japanese rice. When Chinese people come, it's Chinese rice. People come from India, the Middle East and from Egypt, from all over, so we have to have all kinds of rice here."

Chef Suki, chef at Masons

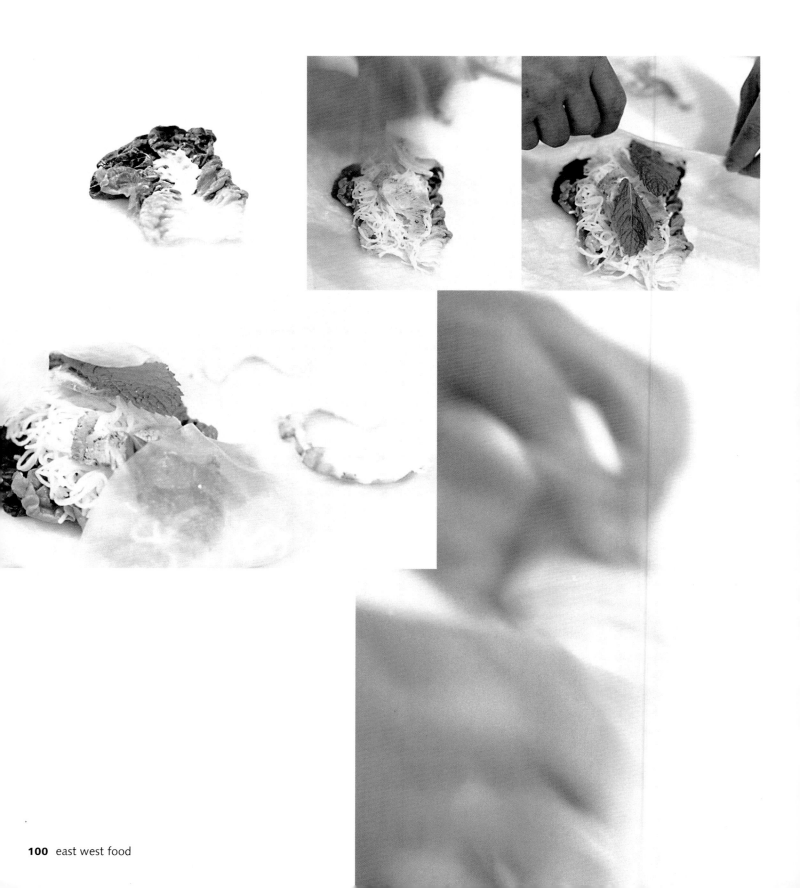

"Personally I'm always going back to history, trying to bring something back and to re-invent something new."

Charles Phan, chef at The Slanted Door

Peanut Sauce

²⁄₃ **cup roasted peanuts**

1–2 small Thai chili peppers, seeded

3 garlic cloves

1 tablespoon sugar

1 tablespoon tomato ketchup

2 tablespoons oyster sauce

½ tablespoon lemon juice

1 cup cooked sweet (glutinous) rice

5 tablespoons miso paste

Spring Rolls

1 piece of lean pork loin, about 8 ounces

ten 12-inch round rice papers

1 head of red-leaf lettuce, leaves separated

½ package thin rice noodles, cooked

15 mint sprigs

10 ounces medium shrimp, cooked, peeled and halved lengthwise

Mayonnaise

2 egg yolks

1 tablespoon white wine vinegar or tarragon vinegar

1 teaspoon Dijon mustard

salt and pepper, to taste

1¼ cups olive oil

1. Start by making the mayonnaise. Put the egg yolks in a bowl with the vinegar and mustard. Add ½ teaspoon of salt and some pepper. Beat to make a smooth paste.

2. Gradually beat in the oil, adding 1 drop at a time at first. When the mixture thickens, pour the oil in a steady stream, beating until all the oil has been added and the mayonnaise is thick.

3. Alternatively, put the egg yolks, vinegar, mustard, salt and pepper in a blender or food processor. Process briefly, then add the oil, drop by drop at first, then in a steady stream until the oil has been incorporated and the mayonnaise is thick.

4. Make the sauce. Combine the peanuts with the chili peppers, garlic and sugar in a food processor and purée to a fine paste.

5. Add the remaining sauce ingredients and continue processing. Add a few tablespoons of water occasionally, to thin the sauce to a smooth and creamy consistency. Set aside.

6. For the spring rolls, put the lean pork in a pan of boiling water and simmer for 10–15 minutes. Thinly slice into 1 x 2-inch pieces.

7. Working with two sheets of rice paper at a time, dip them into a bowl of warm water. Quickly remove and spread out flat on the tabletop, stacking one on top of the other.

8. Lay a leaf of lettuce over the bottom third of the rice paper (the lettuce size should be about 2 x 4 inches). Put a teaspoon of mayonnaise on top of the lettuce. Lay a small amount of rice noodles on top of the lettuce and then 3 pieces of pork and 3 mint sprigs.

9. Fold the left and right side over the filling. Roll up the paper halfway into a cylinder. Lay three shrimp halves, cut side up, along the crease, then keep rolling the paper up into a cylinder. Place the rolls on a platter and cover with a damp tea towel so they stay moist. Repeat the process until you have five spring rolls. Refrigerate any remaining mayonnaise.

10. Cut the spring rolls crosswise and serve with the peanut dipping sauce.

Serves 4–6

Charles Phan at The Slanted Door

Spring Rolls with Peanut Sauce

RICE PAPER

Rice papers are thin sheets made from a paste, which is created by combining rice flour and water. The sheets are then cut into rounds. Rice paper rounds are very brittle when dry, and are softened by being dipped in, or brushed with, water. This makes them malleable and ready for their most common use, in Vietnamese spring rolls.

"My food is a combination of influences, from tradition and flavors. A lot is from my memory and from what it was like when I was growing up. For instance we serve a crêpe. That's what I think of eating in Vietnam. It's a street food of Vietnam, so obviously when I had the restaurant I decided to serve that. In that sense you can say that tradition influences what I do here, and, yes, being here twenty years has influenced me quite a bit. We have a grilled tuna that is not very Vietnamese but it's a local, gorgeous tuna and I love tuna. We make a Vietnamese ginger dipping sauce to go with that. So the local ingredient dictates the direction I'm going, and the kind of food I serve, and the tradition dictates a lot of the taste and the style of cooking."

Charles Phan, chef at The Slanted Door

"In my travels I have picked up a knowledge of different flavors from various countries. I have melted all the flavors together, none of them should fight each other. In this world there are a lot of complementary flavors from different continents."

Chef Suki, chef at Masons

Seared Tuna au Poivre
with Lemongrass Risotto

1 tablespoon black peppercorns

1 tablespoon cilantro seeds

four 6-ounce tuna steaks

½ teaspoon salt

1 tablespoon oil

1 bunch cilantro, separated into long sprigs,
   to garnish

Lemongrass Risotto

3 tablespoons canola oil

1 large onion, diced

1 carrot, diced

1 stalk celery, diced

1⅔ cups arborio rice

6 cups fish stock or bottled clam juice

¾ cup dry white wine

3 stalks lemongrass, cut into large chunks

¼ cup fish sauce

1. Start by making the risotto. Heat the canola oil in a large non-reactive saucepan. Add the onion, carrot and celery and cook over high heat for about 3 minutes. Add the rice and sauté for 2 minutes longer.

2. In another large saucepan, bring the fish stock just to a boil, reduce the heat to very low and keep warm.

3. Add the white wine and lemongrass to the rice mixture. Stir until the wine is absorbed into the rice.

4. Add 1 cup of the stock to the rice and cook over moderate heat, stirring frequently, until absorbed. Continue adding the stock, about ½ cup at a time, stirring constantly until all has been absorbed before adding more. Cook until the rice is just tender, about 25 minutes. Stir in the fish sauce. If the risotto is too sticky, add a little more stock. Cover with a lid and remove from the heat. Reserve. (Remove the lemongrass before serving if you like.)

5. Crush the peppercorns and cilantro seeds separately using a pestle and mortar or with the back of a sauté pan on a chopping board. Crush the seeds until cracked but not as far as a powder. Season the fish with salt and coat with the crushed spices.

5. Heat the oil in a heavy sauté pan until very hot. Sear both sides of the tuna for about 2 minutes on each side or to desired doneness.

6. Serve the seared tuna with the risotto, garnished with cilantro sprigs and with fresh vegetables of your choice.

Serves 4

Kirk Webber at Cafe Kati

"If you have got a choice of all these different grains, different noodles and different rices, then there is so much more you can do."

Chris Benians, chef at The Collection

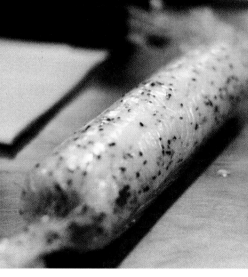

"Certain styles of cuisine have different forms of starches. All of them are a lot more flavorsome and lighter than potato."

Chris Benians, chef at The Collection

Lobster Sushi

1. Put the rice in a sieve and wash under cold running water for a few minutes. Soak in a bowl of cold water for about 1 hour, changing the water frequently, then wash again for a few minutes until the water runs clear.

2. Place the rice in a saucepan with a tight fitting lid, add the measured water and bring to a boil. Place a clean damp cloth over the pan to form a seal and cover once again with the lid. Remove from the heat and leave for 15 minutes.

3. Transfer the rice to a large metal bowl, pour in half the vinegar and mix it into the rice using a firm spatula, adding the rest of the vinegar at the end but ensuring that the mixture is not too sloppy. While you are doing this you will need someone to fan the rice to cool it down quickly. Alternatively place a larger bowl, full of of ice, under the rice bowl while you cut in the vinegar. When cool and glossy, cover the rice with a damp cloth until you have your other ingredients ready.

4. Bring a large pan of water to the boil and cook the lobster until done, 3–4 minutes, remove the lobster from the pan and cool in a bowl of iced water to stop it from cooking any further. Remove all the meat from the lobster and cut it into ¼-inch chunks.

5. Cut two sheets of plastic wrap just larger than the sheets of nori. Using a palette knife dipped in cold water, press the rice into two squares on the plastic wrap, making the rice squares the same size as the nori. Set aside.

6. Place a sheet of nori on a bamboo rolling mat and top with half of the lobster, samphire, cucumber and mooli, making an even layer over the entire sheet. Roll up the filling ingredients using the mat and wetting the edge of the nori with your fingers to make it stick. The roll should be 1–1½ inches thick.

7. Place a rice square on the rolling mat and lay the lobster roll along one end of it. Roll up the rice using the rolling mat to enclose the filling ingredients and removing the plastic wrap. Roll the whole thing in half the sesame seeds. Wrap this up tightly in a clean piece of plastic wrap to make cutting easier. Repeat the whole process with the remaining ingredients to make a second roll. Remove the plastic wrap and slice across into pieces.

8. Serve with a bowl of soy sauce and chopsticks. Remember to eat sushi as soon as you make it for best results and don't be tempted to put it in the refrigerator, as it won't taste as good.

Serves 4

Chris Benians and Cass Titcombe at The Collection

Rice

1 cup Japanese short-grain rice

1¼ cups water

3–4 tablespoons seasoned rice vinegar

soy sauce, to serve

Sushi

1 lobster

2 sheets nori (seaweed)

2 ounces samphire, blanched

2 ounces cucumber, julienned

2 ounces mooli (page 175), peeled and julienned

⅔ cup sesame seeds, toasted (use a mixture of light and dark seeds)

"A very simple yet elegant canapé – originally designed for guests who wanted a scallop canapé with a twist. For me it was a different way to use the glutinous black rice that is most often used to make a sticky sweet rice pudding. At Chinois I tend to use the local bay scallops; they are beautiful to eat. Wash and clean the scallops, remove the muscle that joins the scallop to the shells, then trim off the roes, which can be used in a soup or marinade or in a multitude of ways. I tend to use Royal Atlantic salmon caviar to top the canapés. This comes fresh from Tasmania and is readily available, the quality being excellent."

Asian Black Rice Blini Canapés

1. Pat the scallops dry and place in a shallow dish. Make a marinade with the lime juice and zest, pepper, wine, olive oil and lemon thyme. Pour the marinade over the scallops and fold through well. Scallops need gentle handling so as not to damage the meat. Let the scallops rest in the marinade for at least 20 minutes.

2. Meanwhile cook the black rice in boiling water until tender. Drain in a colander and rinse under running water.

3. Make the blini mixture by combining the flour, milk, egg yolks and seasoning to taste, mixing well until smooth. Fold in the cooked rice and green onions.

4. Whisk the egg whites to soft peaks and then fold into the rice mixture.

5. Heat a heavy frying pan and lightly oil it. Add a few teaspoons of the blini mixture to make a few blinis at a time. Cook to golden on both sides to ensure even cooking. Transfer to a large platter and keep warm while making the remaining blinis and cooking the scallops.

6. Drain scallops and just brown the outsides, either on a very hot grill or griddle or under a very hot broiler for under a minute. Remove and lay flat on a plate.

7. To assemble the canapé, place a tiny dollop of seasoned mayonnaise on each blini, then place a Vietnamese mint leaf on each, followed by a scallop. Spoon a small amount of caviar over each scallop and serve.

Makes 24 blinis, any extras are for personal sampling!

Stanislaus Soares at Chinois

Scallops
24 scallops
juice and zest of 1 lime
¼ teaspoon freshly ground pepper
2 tablespoons dry white wine
1 tablespoon extra-virgin olive oil
2 sprigs lemon thyme, finely chopped

Blinis
½ cup glutinous black rice
⅔ cup all-purpose flour
¾ cup milk
2 eggs, separated
salt and pepper, to taste
2 green onions, finely sliced whites and green
2 teaspoons olive oil

To Serve
4 tablespoons seasoned mayonnaise
Vietnamese mint
salmon caviar

"This one is something different for us Westerners, it's called congee and is a staple food in China and other parts of Asia. You can really put what ever you want into it; so use up any leftovers you have left, like herbs, vegetables, fish or meat. Congees are light, tasty and appetizing."

Shiitake Mushroom and Tofu Congee

10 ounces pork, minced

1 cup glutinous white rice

6 cups white stock (can be fish, pork, chicken or vegetable)

oil for deep-frying

4 ounces tofu, sliced

salt, to taste

½ tablespoon sesame oil

3½ ounces shiitake mushrooms, sliced

3½ ounces green beans, sliced at an angle and blanched

2 green onions, julienned

1 chili pepper, julienned

2 tablespoons cilantro leaves

1. Tie the pork in a piece of cheesecloth.

2. Wash and drain the rice thoroughly, place in a large pan with the stock and the pork, bring to a boil and cook until done, 20-25 minutes.

3. Meanwhile, heat the oil to 350–375°F, or until a cube of bread browns in 30 seconds. Add the tofu and fry until golden. Cut into julienne strips and place in four bowls.

4. When the rice and pork are cooked (it is now congee), drain off any fat, remove and discard the cheesecloth, and pour the congee over the tofu.

5. In a frying pan, sauté the mushrooms in the sesame oil until golden. Mix the mushrooms, green beans, green onions, chili and cilantro together and pour over the rice. Adjust the seasoning, then serve. To make a slightly runny congee, add more stock just before serving.

Serves 4

Graham Harris at Cicada

a dash of
citrus

Lemons, limes, oranges and grapefruit all add a wonderfully tangy taste to food, similar in some ways to that of vinegar, but fresher.

Lime is probably the most frequently used citrus fruit for East-West food and grapefruit the least, although both pink and white grapefruits are used in salads.

All parts of citrus fruits can be used – the rind or zest, juice and segments – and each adds an individual taste to a dish. Often when the segments of oranges or grapefruits are used, the skin or membrane between the segments is removed. This means the fruit imparts juice and flavor to the rest of the dish, and that the fruit melts in the mouth to release even more flavor.

Lemons and limes add similar flavors to dishes, although the lime has a greater acidity and sharpness, and its flavors, particularly that of the juice, always come through more sharply in a dish.

In Asia, the considerable use of citrus fruits is not thought to be exotic. They are an accepted part of the culture and cuisine. Dishes involving citrus fruit can be sweet, tart, bitter or sharp, but after cooking and when used together with herbs and spices, these dishes can be smooth, with just a hint of acidity.

Citrus juice can be used instead of vinegar. Lemon juice is quite frequently used in salad dressings, and any sort of citrus juice also makes a welcome companion to a deep-fried dish. Lemon or lime juice or zest adds an edge to other ingredients without becoming an overly prominent taste, and, to complete the citric experience, fresh lemonade, often garnished with limes, is a refreshing drink to accompany any meal.

"We use a lot, a lot of lime juice. It depends on what cuisine. If we're doing Thai or Vietnamese, they need a lot of citrus juice. While the Chinese would use vinegar, the Japanese would probably use vinegar and lemon or lime juice, but a lot of citrus."

Barney Brown, chef at Betelnut

"It's only recently that people are thinking 'Oh, why don't I combine some of these Italian ingredients with some Indian ingredients.' I think the main reason for this is that a lot more people, especially chefs, are traveling and they're impressed with the food they find overseas. When people go to the New World, which has only recently been recognized for its wines, they discover there is some really interesting food there, too. Chefs can get a bit bored in their work, like anyone else, and are often looking for the next big influence. We're now seeing Asian-influenced food creeping onto established menus, alongside fantastic wine lists, which finally gives it a well-deserved credibility. The old fallacy that beer is the only thing to drink with spicy food, especially chili-based dishes, is finally being dispelled."

Peter Gordon, chef at The Sugar Club

The Sugar Club

This captivating restaurant is located in what, not so many years ago, was a drug pushers' street in Notting Hill, London. Any idea of this certainly doesn't deter people now, and the convivial and welcoming atmosphere makes a visit to this restaurant a real pleasure. The Sugar Club is cool, trendy and confident, with a fantastic reputation; but it is not imposing.

   The chef at The Sugar Club, Peter Gordon, creates his fusion food in various ways (see also *The Sugar Club Cookbook*, Hodder and Stoughton, 1997). The take on the food can be looking at a remake of a traditional dish or encompassing traditional elements of the East and West (and the southern hemisphere). Peter creates altogether new dishes, which include some well-known ingredients. The challenge to the palate is an extremely pleasurable one. This is food that melts in your mouth and makes you want to carry on eating.

Roast Carrot, Olive,
Cilantro and Lemon Salad with Grilled Squid

"This is a quick and simple dish, which is a great accompaniment to squid. I also use the salad with other fish and occasionally meats. It brings together a lot of disparate ingredients from several areas."

4 large carrots, peeled and cut on an angle into oval rings, ¼ inch wide

2 red onions, cut into rings

16 green olives

12 cilantro seeds, lightly crushed

1 small lemon, cut into ¼-inch dice, seeds removed

2 tablespoons cold-pressed sesame oil

3 tablespoons sunflower oil

2 tablespoons fish sauce

1 cup cilantro

For the Squid

4 squid, cleaned

2–3 tablespoons sesame oil (optional)

1. Preheat the oven to 400°F. Mix together all of the salad ingredients except the cilantro leaves and place in a baking dish. Cover with foil and roast in the middle of the oven for 20 minutes. Remove the foil, stir well, cover the dish again and roast for a further 15 minutes. Remove the foil and continue cooking until the carrots start to caramelize. Remove from the oven and leave to cool, then stir in the cilantro leaves.

2. To cook the squid, either place on a grill or fry in a wok with the sesame oil for 1–2 minutes.

3. To assemble, spoon the salad and any juices onto a plate and top with the grilled squid.

Serves 4

Peter Gordon at The Sugar Club

"I tend to 'borrow' techniques that take my fancy, forego the ones that don't work for me or adapt them so they do. I love to try new ways of cooking, of course, as this is always very stimulating and creative, but I do have a tendency to return to the oldies and the goodies."

Michael Lee-Richards, chef at Michael's

"One utensil I would definitely not be without would be my trusty birch whisk. Or a zester. I quite fancy my blowtorch as well, for caramelizing the sugar on top of brûlées or finishing off the tops of batch meringues. And while I think about it, my little handheld blender has saved many a sagging sauce!"

Michael Lee-Richards, chef at Michael's

Marmalade Chicken
with Stacked Walnut Rice

6 chicken leg and thigh portions, skinned

salt and pepper, to taste

4 tablespoons extra-thick-cut marmalade, chopped

1 small bunch mint, leaves chopped

3 garlic cloves, finely chopped

grated zest and juice of 1 large orange

2 tablespoons butter, softened

handful of chopped herbs, such as parsley, mint or chervil, to garnish

Sauce

2 teaspoons cornstarch

scant 2 cups chicken stock

sugar, to taste (optional)

Stacked Walnut Rice

1 tablespoon olive oil

1 small onion, finely chopped

½ cup coarsely chopped walnuts

1½ cups short-grain rice, cooked

1 egg white, lightly beaten

salt and pepper, to taste

1. Preheat the oven to 350°F. Sprinkle the chicken pieces with salt and pepper all over, then arrange them in a roasting pan in a single layer.

2. In a bowl, combine the marmalade with the mint, garlic, orange zest and butter. (Keep the orange juice for the sauce.) Season with salt and pepper. Blend the mixture together until thoroughly mixed, then spread all over the chicken pieces.

3. Roast the chicken on the top rack of the oven for about 40 minutes, checking the chicken after 30 minutes, or until cooked through, basting once with the pan juices.

4. Remove the pan from the oven and transfer the chicken to a serving dish. Keep warm while making the sauce and the rice. Leave the oven turned on.

5. Skim off any fat from the pan juices by tilting the roasting pan so the liquid flows into the corner; use a large spoon to take off the surface fat.

6. In a small bowl, blend the orange juice with the cornstarch until smooth. Add the juice mixture and the stock to the roasting pan and stir well to blend with the pan juices. Bring to a boil over medium heat, stirring all the time. Simmer for 10 minutes, then taste and check for seasoning, perhaps adding a dash of sugar. Keep warm while making the walnut rice.

7. To make the rice, heat the olive oil in a sauté pan. Add the onion and sauté for about 5 minutes until softened and lightly browned. Stir in the walnuts and cook for a few minutes longer.

8. Remove from the heat and stir in the rice to mix thoroughly. Fold in the egg white and season well with salt and pepper.

9. Increase the oven to 400°F. To serve, shape the rice into six squares on a baking sheet. Put into the hot oven to heat through. When firm enough to handle, slide the squares onto warmed plates. Place a chicken piece on top and pour the sauce all over. Dust generously with fresh herbs and serve at once.

Serves 6

Michael Lee-Richards at Michael's

SEVILLE ORANGES

Marmalade is most often made using Seville oranges, which have a bitter-sour taste.

CB: I would definitely use a lime rather then a lemon, but it does depend upon the dish.

CT: We couldn't do without limes.

CB: A lot of this food is Japanese, with a sort of citrus vinegar and that's lime, lemon and orange – like a satsuma and that's nice and citrusy. We use that a lot in dressings and stuff, mixing lemon and lime. It's not quite the same, it's got just a little bit of something extra.

Chris Benians and Cass Titcombe, chefs at The Collection

Miso and Lime-baked Salmon
with Sugar Snaps, Soybeans and Red Ginger

1. Remove any bones from the salmon with a pair of tweezers and scrape off any remaining scales. Slice thinly into twelve pieces, cutting into the fish at an angle.

2. Mix the sake, miso, honey, garlic and lime juice together in a small bowl. Place the fish in a shallow dish and pour over half of the marinade, making sure everything is well covered. Wrap with plastic wrap and marinate overnight if possible.

3. Blanch the sugar snaps in boiling water for about 45 seconds, then remove with a slotted spoon, refresh in iced water and drain well. Blanch the shelled soybeans in the boiling water as well. Refresh them in iced water as well, to prevent discoloring.

4. Preheat the oven to 450°F. Place the fish on a baking sheet in a single layer and cook in the hot oven for 2–3 minutes.

5. Heat up a wok, add the oil and stir-fry the sugar snaps, soybeans and ginger until they are hot. Add the soy sauce and toss to coat lightly, then divide among four plates. Place three slices of salmon on each plate and drizzle the remaining sauce over the plates. Serve with a wedge of lime. You could sprinkle over some black sesame seeds, if you wish.

Serves 4

Chris Benians and Cass Titcombe at The Collection

1½-pound piece of salmon fillet

7 tablespoons sake

6 tablespoons miso

2 tablespoons clear honey

1 garlic clove, crushed

2 limes, 1 juiced and 1 quartered

1 pound sugar snap peas

1 pound fresh soybeans, shelled

1 tablespoon canola oil

2 tablespoons sliced red pickled ginger

1 tablespoon soy sauce

black sesame seeds, to serve (optional)

"I love the mixture of the beautiful tangy taste of lime juice, cilantro and chili. This dish is a perfect combination of all those wonderful flavors, ones that get your taste buds going. In short, it's happy food!"

Prawn Salad

28 tiger prawns, peeled and deveined

banana leaf squares (optional)

1 green papaya, peeled and finely julienned

2 unripe or green mangoes (as firm as possible), peeled and finely julienned

Dressing

8 limes, cut in half and juiced

2 red chilies, finely diced

2 dried chilies, crushed

3 tablespoons fish sauce, or to taste

1 teaspoon sugar, or to taste

Garnish

1 cup cilantro

1 cup Thai basil leaves

1. Combine all the ingredients for the dressing, then adjust the taste to hot, sour or sweet, as you wish.

2. Either grill or dry-fry the prawns in a wok. Cook until just opaque. Set aside for a few moments.

3. To serve, mix the papaya and mangoes together with the prawns and a little dressing. Place a banana leaf square in the center of each of four plates, then place a serving of the papaya and mango mixture on top. Garnish with a drizzle of dressing and the cilantro and Thai basil.

Serves 4

Graham Harris at Cicada

Lime and Coconut Parfait

1. Make the parfait. In a bowl whisk the egg yolks with an electric whisk, until thick and pale. Combine the sugar and measured water in a saucepan and boil until it reaches 250°F. Pour the hot syrup into the egg mixture slowly, whisking all the time. Add the lime zest and juice.

2. Whip the cream to soft peaks and carefully fold in the coconut milk, then fold into the egg mixture together with the malibu. Line a terrine with plastic wrap and pour in the parfait mixture. Cover with plastic wrap and freeze for at least 6 hours.

3. Preheat the oven to 225°F. Shave the coconut with a mandoline or a potato peeler and place on a baking sheet. Place in the oven for 20–25 minutes.

4. Put all the sauce ingredients in a saucepan, bring to the boil and simmer until it has reduced and is thick.

5. To serve, remove the parfait from the freezer, dip the terrine into a bowl of hot water for a few seconds and then turn out on to a platter. Cut it into 8–10 slices and serve with a drizzle of lime sauce and a mound of grated coconut on top of each serving.

Serves 8–10

Chris Benians and Cass Titcombe at The Collection

Parfait

13 egg yolks

1½ cups superfine sugar

¼ cup water

zest and juice of 3 limes

1¾ cups heavy cream

1¼ cups canned coconut milk

¼ cup malibu (coconut-flavored white rum)

Sauce

7 tablespoons lime juice

½ cup sugar

¾ cup plus 2 tablespoons water

half a fresh coconut, grated, to garnish

"This combination has worked wonderfully at Chinois, the flavors tend to lend and blend together beautifully. As a dish it's very visual. We use Royal Tasmanian Atlantic salmon as it's available fresh every day; the taste is just superb. This quantity provides four generous portions."

Grilled Salmon
with Spinach Gnocchi and a Kaffir Lime Leaf Sauce

1. Start by making the sauce. Cover the salmon bones with water, bring to a boil, then reduce the heat and simmer gently to make a rich fish stock.

2. Strain the bones, then return the stock to the pan and boil to reduce the fish stock down to about 1¼ cups.

3. Reduce the heat to low and add the cubed butter, stirring constantly. Be careful not to let this return to a boil or your sauce will split. Add the chopped kaffir lime leaves together with the grated zest and juice and the chopped chili pepper.

4. To cook the salmon, remove any tiny bones from the fish with tweezers. Cut the fish into four equal portions.

5. In a shallow dish, marinate the fish in a mixture of sake, mirin, soy sauce and lemon zest and juice. Take care not to let the fish stay in this marinade for more than 30–35 minutes, for the fish tends to "cook" in the marinade.

6. While the fish is marinating, make the gnocchi. Mix all the ingredients together until well blended. Form into small balls.

7. Bring a large pan of salted water to a boil. Roll the gnocchi balls lightly in a little extra flour, then mark with the tines of a fork. Drop the gnocchi into the boiling water, wait for them to come to the surface, then drain and toss in butter.

8. Remove the fish from the marinade and pat dry with paper towels. Prepare a fire in a grill, and cook the salmon on both sides for only about 7 minutes altogether or it will get too dry.

9. To serve, place the salmon on the hot buttered gnocchi, pour the sauce over and garnish with chive flowers.

Serves 4

Stanislaus Soares at Chinois

Salmon

2 pounds salmon fillet without skin, bones reserved

7 tablespoons sake

6 tablespoons mirin

¼ cup soy sauce

grated zest and juice of 1 lemon

chive flowers, to garnish

Gnocchi

7 ounces potatoes, peeled, cooked and mashed

½ cup cooked chopped spinach

2 egg yolks

⅔ cup all-purpose flour, plus extra for coating

1 tablespoon butter, plus extra for tossing

salt and pepper, to taste

¼ teaspoon ground nutmeg

Sauce

salmon bones

water

7 tablespoons cold butter, cut into cubes

5 teaspoons finely chopped kaffir lime leaves

⅓ teaspoon grated zest and juice of 1 kaffir lime

1 small green chili pepper, seeded and finely chopped

a pinch of
herb
and spice

The use of herbs and spices can alter any dish.

They can retain the authenticity or make the difference. The flavors of many herbs are so well known that it is important to recognize those tastes before experimenting. Both herbs and spices can be overpowering if used in indiscreet quantities. It is because of their distinct tastes that herbs and spices make such a difference.

Herbs add scent, flavor and often color when used in cooking. Their flavor comes from the essential oils that are stored in the leaves, stems and flowers. There are well-recognized uses of herbs: basil with tomato and tarragon with chicken, for instance. What makes herbs so essential to cooking is that those and other classic combinations can be interchanged and expanded upon. The exploration of herbs encourages their cultivation.

Spices are mostly not fresh. They are dried and aromatic. They can be sticks, pods and seeds of different shapes and sizes, and they can nearly all be ground. Once ground, spices lose their smell and taste quickly, so it is best to grind them as and when needed. Strangely, the term "spicy" is often used to give the idea of heat; it does not necessarily involve spices.

Spices too have classic combinations, but these are probably not as traditional as those of herbs. The uses of spices and spice mixtures vary from region to region and from one cook to the next.

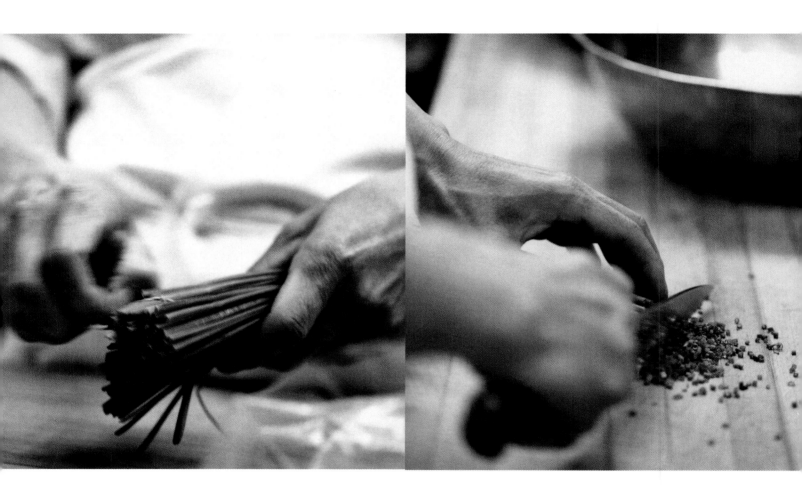

"Anything that kind of packs a wallop in a sense has influenced me. It could be a blend of spices, like a blend of garam masala from India or like the garam masala I did on the last menu. We did a great prawn satay on that

menu, it was like a Thai satay, and it had a Malaysian marinade on it with Indian spices. A kind of marriage of Indian and Chinese and Thai, which I see happening in Malaysia."

Kirk Webber, chef at Cafe Kati

1. Start by making the candied pecans. Preheat the oven to 325°F. Whisk the egg whites in a large bowl, until soft peaks form. While whisking, slowly add the sugar and salt. Continue whisking for about 2 minutes longer.

2. Add the pecans and gently fold into the egg white mixture. Spread the pecan mixture on an ungreased baking sheet. Bake in the oven for 15 minutes or until the egg whites are puffed and golden brown.

3. Meanwhile, make the dressing. Place all the dressing ingredients in a bowl and whisk until combined.

4. Remove the pecans from the oven and toss to deflate the egg whites, spread out again, return to the oven and bake for about 15 minutes longer or until the nuts are lightly toasted.

5. In a large bowl, combine the cabbage with the jicama, grapefruit, ½ cup of the candied pecans, shallot oil, rau ram or mint and enough dressing to coat lightly. Store the remaining pecans in an airtight jar for later use. Reserve any remaining dressing for later use as well.

6. Toss all the ingredients together well and serve at once.

Serves 6

Charles Phan at The Slanted Door

1 pound red cabbage, shredded

8 ounces jicama, shredded

1 large grapefruit, peeled and segmented

1 tablespoon shallot-flavored oil

4 tablespoons chopped rau ram or mint

Dressing

3 garlic cloves, minced

2–3 Thai chili peppers, seeded and minced

6 tablespoons rice vinegar

¾ cup light soy sauce

6 tablespoons sugar

½ cup water

Candied Pecans

4 egg whites

½ cup sugar

¼ teaspoon salt

2½ cups pecan halves

Grapefruit Salad with Jicama

JICAMA

This vegetable is also known as yam bean, sweet turnip and Mexican potato. It has a pale brown skin that, when peeled, reveals white, crisp flesh. It can be eaten raw or cooked, sliced, diced or shredded. Its raw taste is nutty and slightly sweet, but, when it is cooked, it takes on the flavors of other ingredients cooked with it. Always peel and cut jicama immediately before use because it discolors quite quickly.

"I do twists on food, but I do try to keep the flavors fairly focused."

Kirk Webber, chef at Cafe Kati

Romaine Lettuce with a Spicy Mango Vinaigrette, Tempura Shrimp and Yellow and Red Beets

1. Slice the cucumber lengthwise into long, thin strips using a mandoline. The slices must be thin enough to curl and wrap the romaine hearts.

2. Make the vinaigrette. Purée the mango with the chili paste, vinegar and mustard in a blender. Slowly add the oil and blend until combined.

3. Toss the lettuce hearts in the vinaigrette. Split each one into four portions, wrap each portion in cucumber slices and secure with a skewer.

4. Peel the beets, then finely shred using a Japanese mandoline if you have one.

5. To make the tempura batter, mix together the cornstarch, flour and baking powder in a medium bowl. Add the oil and enough water to make a smooth, runny batter. Season with salt and pepper.

6. Heat the oil in a deep frying pan or wok to 350–375°F, or until a cube of bread browns in 30 seconds. Dip the shrimp in the flour and then into the tempura batter. Fry until crisp, turning occasionally.

7. To serve, divide the lettuce hearts and shrimp evenly among four plates. Garnish with the beets and any remaining vinaigrette.

Serves 4

Kirk Webber at Cafe Kati

JAPANESE MANDOLINE

The Japanese mandoline is a very fast and effective way of slicing or shredding hard fruits and vegetables. It is an invaluable piece of equipment for chefs. A mandoline rests on a slant away from the user and has one or several blades, which are adjustable for thickness. It is important for safety to push the ingredient you are slicing away from you. It is also easier to use the mandoline this way.

1 cucumber
2 romaine lettuce hearts
1 red and 1 yellow beet
oil for frying
16 large shrimp, peeled and butterflied
3 tablespoons all-purpose flour

Spicy Mango Vinaigrette
⅓ cup diced ripe mango
1 teaspoon chili paste
¼ cup balsamic vinegar
1 tablespoon Dijon mustard
2 tablespoons olive oil

Tempura Batter
⅓ cup cornstarch
¼ cup all-purpose flour
1 teaspoon baking powder
2 tablespoons oil
approximately ¾ cup sparkling water
salt and pepper, to taste

"Here a mad mixture of herbs and spices from all over the world is used to lift the flavors of an Australian meat and a European potato."

Marinated and Seared Kangaroo Loin

with Spice-roasted Potatoes and Arugula

4 kangaroo loins, 7–10 ounces each

12-14 ounces new potatoes, scrubbed to remove all dirt

7 tablespoons extra-virgin olive oil

5 whole star anise, finely ground

2 teaspoons sweet paprika

2 teaspoons fennel seeds

¼ cup lime juice

7 tablespoons water

1 teaspoon coriander seeds, finely ground

3 tablespoons sesame oil, plus a little for brushing

4 ounces arugula leaves

¼ cup extra virgin olive oil

2 tablespoons balsamic vinegar

Marinade

2 tablespoons fresh rosemary leaves

2 tablespoons fresh oregano leaves

2 tablespoons fresh thyme leaves

2 garlic cloves, finely chopped

2 kaffir lime leaves, finely shredded

1 teaspoon cumin seeds

2 tablespoons tamari soy sauce

1. Start by making the marinade. Finely chop the herbs and mix with the garlic, kaffir lime leaves, cumin and tamari. Add the kangaroo to this and mix well. Place in a shallow dish, cover and marinate in the refrigerator overnight, turning twice during this time.

2. The next day, preheat the oven to 400°F. Heat a roasting pan in the oven. Once the pan is warm, place the potatoes in it and mix with the remaining ingredients except for the arugula, olive oil and balsamic vinegar. Roast for 40 minutes, stirring from time to time. The potatoes should be just cooked by this time; if not, continue cooking until done and before starting the next step.

3. Heat a heavy frying pan until smoking. Rub the marinade off the kangaroo and stir half of it into the roasting potatoes as they are cooking. Discard the remainder of the marinade.

4. Brush the kangaroo loins with a little sesame oil, then, in the hot frying pan, sear on all sides to a light brown.

5. Place the loins on top of the potatoes and roast for a further 5–10 minutes. Note that as kangaroo is a very lean meat, it should only be cooked rare to medium-rare or else it will be overdone and tough. The final cooking time will depend on the size of the loins.

6. Remove the meat from the oven and let it rest in a warm place for 5 minutes before slicing. Make sure you slice it against the grain.

7. Toss the arugula with half the olive oil and all of the balsamic vinegar and arrange on plates. Spoon the roasted potatoes on top and then the slices of kangaroo. Drizzle with the remaining olive oil.

Serves 4

Peter Gordon at The Sugar Club

TAMARI SOY SAUCE
Tamari is a rich, dark, wheat-free soy sauce traditionally made from fermented soybeans.

"Live scallops are the best to use in this salad, but if they are not available the shelled ones are fine. Ponzu sauce contains citrus juices and is sold in Asian supermarkets. If it is not available, you can replace it with equal quantities of lemon and lime juice."

Warm Scallop Salad
with Ponzu Dressing

1. Remove the scallops from the shells and discard everything except the white meat. Refrigerate the scallops for about 24 hours so they will become firm.

2. Make the dressing by combining all the ingredients in a small saucepan and gently bringing the mixture barely to a boil. Remove from the heat and allow the ingredients to cool and blend together. Strain through a fine sieve and set aside.

3. Slice each scallop into four slices and lay the slices in a single layer on a baking sheet.

4. Heat the oil in a deep-fat fryer to 325°F. Working in batches, deep-fry the sweet potato in the hot oil until crisp but not colored. Drain on paper towels.

5. Trim and core the fennel. Cut into very thin slices with a mandoline and place in ice water.

6. Blanch the peas in boiling water for about 1 minute. Drain and refresh under cold water. Cut lengthwise into very thin strips.

7. Drain the fennel and toss with the mooli, cucumber, peas and green onions in a large bowl.

8. Preheat the broiler until very hot and warm the dressing slightly. Pour a little of the dressing over the sliced scallops. Cook the scallops under the broiler for 1–2 minutes, being careful not to allow them to overcook.

9. To serve, line four plates with mizuna leaves, then place a little of the salad on each plate with some crisp sweet potato. Top with four slices of scallop on each plate. Cover with more salad, then four more scallop slices and continue until each plate has twelve scallop slices. Drizzle the remaining dressing over the salad and finally sprinkle with the black sesame seeds.

Serves 4

Chris Benians and Cass Titcombe at The Collection

12 live scallops in the shell
sunflower oil for deep-frying
1 large orange sweet potato, peeled and
   julienned
1 fennel bulb
2 ounces sugar snap peas
3½ ounces mooli (page 175), peeled and
   julienned
½ small cucumber, seeded and julienned
1 bunch green onions, white only, thinly sliced
2 handfuls of mizuna leaves
black sesame seeds

Ponzu Dressing
¼ cup ponzu sauce
2 tablespoons fish sauce
2 tablespoons rice vinegar
1 tablespoon sesame oil
1 tablespoon pickled ginger juice or
   1 or 2 slices pickled ginger
1 whole star anise
10 cilantro seeds
10 white peppercorns
pinch cumin seeds

MIZUNA
This salad leaf is not widely available, but it is gradually becoming more common. It originates from China and has been cultivated in Japan for many years. The leaves having a mild mustardy flavor; the stalks are crisp, white and succulent.

Crispy Wrapped Beef

4 thin slices beef sirloin, about 3 ounces
   each
four 9-inch spring roll wrappers
five-spice powder
1 cup cooked glass noodles (mung bean
   threads)
4 green onions, 2 julienned and 2 finely
   chopped
1 bunch cilantro, leaves only
1 egg, beaten
vegetable oil for frying
juice of 1 lime
Asian salad leaves, to serve

Sweet Chili Sauce
4 red bird's eye chili peppers, seeded
1 red pepper, seeded
3 garlic cloves
1 shallot
one 14-ounce can tomatoes
6 tablespoons sugar
5 tablespoons rice vinegar
1 teaspoon salt

1. Start by making the sweet chili sauce. In a food processor, finely chop the chili peppers, pepper, garlic and shallot. Transfer to a saucepan and stir in the tomatoes together with the sugar, vinegar and salt. Bring to a boil, then reduce the heat to very low, cover with a lid and simmer gently for about 1 hour. Remove from the heat and purée in a food processor or blender. Allow to cool.

2. Working with one slice of beef at a time, place it between two pieces of waxed paper and pound it with a meat mallet or rolling pin until it is very thin.

3. Lay out one spring roll wrapper and cover with a slice of beef. Sprinkle it with five-spice powder, then top with some glass noodles, the julienned green onions and a few cilantro leaves. Repeat with the remaining spring roll wrappers, beef, noodles and vegetables.

4. Brush the edges of the wrapper with the beaten egg and roll up tightly, folding over the corners first.

5. Heat the oil in a deep pan to 350–375°F, or until a cube of bread browns in 30 seconds. Deep-fry the spring rolls until golden and crisp. Drain on paper towels.

6. Chop the remaining cilantro leaves and stir into the sweet chili sauce with the chopped green onions and the lime juice.

7. To serve, cut each spring roll diagonally in half and serve with some Asian salad leaves surrounded by some sweet chili sauce.

Serves 4

Chris Benians and Cass Titcombe at The Collection

The Collection

Chris Benians made his mark at Daphne's and now, together with Cass Titcombe, has moved on to something altogether new at The Collection. The Collection is located in one of the smartest areas of London, and its diners are very knowledgeable. The restaurant is named such because it is a collection of foods from all over the world.

For a long time the location the restaurant occupies was an open gallery space used for design-degree shows and for The Conran Shop furniture sale, among other things. Now completely changed and with two huge kitchens installed, there are two distinct areas. The downstairs is more of a brasserie-bar area, with the smarter dining area upstairs. The whole place is beautiful and the precision used in the laying of the tables just adds to the beauty. The climax to this presentation is the food: it looks and tastes amazing.

> "It wasn't really a conscious decision to start creating fusion food. I would say it was just the fact that we wanted to do lots of little bits of everything. So the idea there was to mix a few things."
>
> Cass Titcombe, chef at The Collection

Pan-fried Foie Gras
with Asian Pear, Bok Choy and Sesame

½ teaspoon ground star anise

½ teaspoon ground cumin

½ teaspoon ground coriander

½ teaspoon pepper

1 tablespoon all-purpose flour

2 tablespoons light vegetable oil

4 slices foie gras, each ½ inch thick

2 bok choy, leaves separated

1 Asian pear, cored and sliced

⅓ cup sesame seeds, toasted

Sauce

7 tablespoons soy sauce

¼ cup ponzu sauce

¼ cup sushi vinegar

2 tablespoons mirin

1 tablespoon cornstarch

1. Combine all the sauce ingredients together in a small saucepan and warm gently, stirring all the time. Remove the pan from the heat and allow to cool a little.

2. Combine the star anise, cumin, cilantro, pepper and flour in a small bowl. Heat a heavy sauté pan until very hot. Add about 1 teaspoon of the vegetable oil. Sprinkle the foie gras slices with the spice mixture on both sides. Sear the slices in the hot pan for about 1 minute on each side, then transfer to a platter and reserve.

3. Remove the pan from the heat and stir in the remaining oil, then transfer all the oil, together with any browned bits in the pan, to a wok. Heat until very hot.

4. Add the bok choy to the wok and stir-fry for a few minutes, until just starting to soften. Add the pear slices with about half of the sauce mixture and cook until the sauce just comes to a boil.

5. Divide the bok choy mixture among four plates and sit a slice of foie gras on top of each plate. Drizzle with the remaining sauce and sprinkle with toasted sesame seeds.

Serves 4

Chris Benians and Cass Titcombe at The Collection

SUSHI VINEGAR AND MIRIN

Sushi vinegar is the ingredient that gives sushi its unmistakable flavor. It is a combination of rice vinegar, sugar and salt; the mixture is sprinkled onto the cooked rice and folded in.

Mirin is a slightly sweet Japanese rice wine, which is used as a cooking wine. Medium-dry sherry or white vermouth is a suitable replacement, if necessary.

"Over the years, I have experimented with many different flavors and combinations. As you do. You could say that I have 'affairs with flavors,' some fleeting and some that have turned into long-term friendships. Some of my liaisons have included beets, cilantro, almonds, and lime."

Michael Lee-Richards, chef at Michael's

Five-spice-marinated Lamb Loin

1. Combine all the marinade ingredients in a saucepan and bring to a boil over moderate heat. Simmer for about 20 minutes, then remove from the heat and allow to cool.

2. Place the lamb in a shallow dish and then pour over the marinade. Cover and marinate, refrigerated, for at least 6 hours.

3. Remove the meat from the marinade and drain well. Season well with salt and pepper. Heat the oil in a very hot pan, add the lamb and sauté, just to sear the outside of the meat.

4. With a long sharp knife, cut the meat from the bones, keeping the meat in one piece. Cook the shiitake mushrooms under a preheated broiler until softened.

5. Spread the mustard and peppercorns all over the meat. Place the shiitake mushrooms over the meat and wrap in the caul fat.

6. Make the ragout. Heat the oil in a flameproof casserole dish and sauté the onion, garlic and peppers until slightly softened. Stir in the diced eggplant, tomatoes and basil and cook together for about 10 minutes. Stir in the cooked white beans and simmer for about 20 minutes longer, or until all the vegetables are very soft.

7. Make the sauce. Thinly shred two of the garlic cloves, leaving the rest whole. Sauté all the garlic in half the butter until golden brown; remove the garlic and reserve. Add the wine with the bay leaf and simmer until reduced by about half. Add the veal stock and reduce slightly. Strain the sauce through a very fine sieve or through a double thickness of cheesecloth into a small saucepan. Add the fresh herbs. Season with salt and pepper and stir in the remaining butter to finish the sauce.

8. Preheat the oven to 425°F. Roast the boneless lamb in the preheated oven on a baking sheet, until cooked rare. Remove from the oven and allow to rest for a few minutes. Lightly sauté the asparagus and zucchini. Keep warm.

9. Just before serving, cut the lamb across into slices. Spoon some of the white bean ragout onto each of four plates. Arrange some of the sliced zucchini and one asparagus around the edge together with the whole sautéd garlic. Lay the lamb slices on the ragout and pour the sauce along the top of the lamb slices. Top with the reserved shredded garlic.

Serves 4

Chef Suki at Masons

2 racks of lamb, trimmed (8 bones each)

3 tablespoons olive oil

12 shiitake mushrooms

1 tablespoon grainy Pommery mustard

1 tablespoon black peppercorns

two 4 x 8-inch pieces of caul fat
  (for wrapping crépinettes)

salt and pepper, to taste

Five-spice Marinade

1 cup hoisin sauce

1⅓ cups chopped green onions

2 tablespoons soy sauce

1 cup dry sherry

2 whole star anise

1 tablespoon five-spice powder

1 tablespoon grated ginger root

White Bean Ragout

2 tablespoons olive oil

1 small onion, diced

1 garlic clove, minced

½ each of small red and green peppers,
  seeded and diced

⅓–½ cup diced eggplant

2 tomatoes, peeled, seeded and diced

2 tablespoons finely shredded basil

1½ cups drained, cooked white beans

Red Wine Herb Sauce

14 garlic cloves

2 tablespoons butter

6 tablespoons Burgundy wine

1 small bay leaf

¾ cup veal stock

⅓ cup each chopped basil, parsley
  and oregano

Vegetables

4 asparagus

1 small zucchini, sliced into half-moons

Tortilla Soup with Chicken Potstickers

Tortilla Soup Base

¾ cup chopped onion

2 tablespoons corn oil

6 tomatoes, peeled, seeded and diced

1 garlic clove, finely chopped

4½ cups chicken stock

1 tablespoon tomato paste

1 bay leaf

1 sprig epazote

½ teaspoon ground cumin

salt and white pepper, to taste

Chicken Potstickers

2 ounces boneless chicken breast, very finely chopped

2 tablespoons chopped chives

1 tablespoon sake

1 teaspoon soy sauce

4 potsticker wrappers (wonton skins)

1 egg white

Garnish

oil for deep-frying

½ cup shredded Cheddar cheese

four 8-inch corn tortillas, cut into strips

1. Sauté the onions in the oil until softened. Add the tomatoes and garlic and cook for about 5 minutes.

2. Stir in the chicken stock with the tomato paste, bay leaf, epazote, cumin and seasoning to taste. Simmer gently for about 30 minutes, stirring occasionally.

3. Strain the soup through a fine sieve into a clean pan.

4. Heat the oil for the garnish to 350–375°F, or until a cube of bread browns in 30 seconds. Add the tortilla strips and deep-fry until crisp. Drain and reserve.

5. In a bowl, combine the chicken with the chives, sake and soy sauce. Divide the mixture evenly among each of the potsticker wrappers. With your finger spread a little of the egg white around the edge of each wrapper and fold in half. Seal the edges together with your fingers.

6. Steam the potstickers for about 5 minutes, until cooked through.

7. Heat the soup through gently and serve with the hot potstickers, garnished with the cheese and deep-fried tortilla crisps.

Serves 4

Chef Suki at Masons

POTSTICKERS

Potsticker wrappers, like wonton skins, are made from noodle dough. They are stuffed, most commonly with meat or fish and sometimes with vegetables.

Green Papaya Salad

2½ cups shredded, peeled green papaya

2 plum tomatoes, thinly sliced

3 ounces cooked baby shrimp (optional)

Dressing

½ teaspoon finely chopped garlic

1 teaspoon finely chopped hot chili peppers

2 tablespoons fish sauce

2 tablespoons lime juice

1 teaspoon chopped cilantro

1 teaspoon chopped Thai basil

1 teaspoon chopped mint

1 teaspoon sugar

1. Combine the grated papaya with the sliced tomatoes and shrimp, if using, in a large bowl.

2. Combine all the dressing ingredients together in a small bowl and whisk until combined.

3. Pour the dressing over the salad and lightly toss to coat evenly.

Serves 4

Barney Brown at Betelnut

Indonesian Chicken Satay

1 pound boneless, skinless chicken thighs,
  cut into ½-inch strips
salad leaves, to serve (optional)

Marinade
2 tablespoons chopped shallot
1½ tablespoons chopped garlic
1½ tablespoons grated palm sugar or
  brown sugar
2 teaspoons ground fennel seeds
2 teaspoons ground cumin
2 teaspoons ground cilantro
2 teaspoons finely chopped lemongrass
2 teaspoons grated ginger root
¼ teaspoon ground turmeric
½ teaspoon salt

Spicy Peanut Sauce
1 tablespoon vegetable oil
2 teaspoons grated ginger root
1 teaspoon finely chopped garlic
1 teaspoon finely chopped lemongrass
2 teaspoons chopped shallot
¼ teaspoon ground turmeric
2 tablespoons ground roasted peanuts
1 tablespoon hot chili sauce (sambal oelek)
1 teaspoon sugar
1 teaspoon fish sauce
1 tablespoon tamarind concentrate or
  lime juice
¼ cup water
½ cup canned coconut milk

1. Make the marinade. Combine all ingredients in a bowl until well mixed. Add enough water to make a smooth paste.
2. Place the chicken in a bowl, add the marinade, cover and marinate in the refrigerator for 4 hours or overnight.
3. Make the sauce. Heat the oil in a small pan and sauté the ginger, garlic, lemongrass and shallots for about 5 minutes or until soft. Add all the remaining ingredients, with only half the coconut milk, cover and cook over a very low heat for about 20 minutes. Adjust the consistency with the remaining coconut milk.
4. Preheat the broiler or prepare a fire in a grill. Remove the chicken from marinade and thread onto bamboo skewers. Broil or grill for a few minutes on each side, until cooked through.
5. Serve the chicken skewers with individual dishes of peanut sauce for dipping and a little salad if wished.
Serves 4–6
Barney Brown at Betelnut

"You get a group of people together and someone wants some Japanese, someone wants some Chinese, somebody wants Vietnamese. So, you get it all under one roof at Betelnut, which is very convenient."

Barney Brown, chef at Betelnut

delicious fish

Fish is increasingly popular and widely recognized for its nutritious qualities.

There are literally hundreds of different types of fish. To start to group them together, there are three basic types into which all fish fit: freshwater fish, round sea fish and flat sea fish. Within each of these categories, there are a number of well-known fish and equally some lesser-known fish. The best way to be sure of getting the fish you want is to specify the type: white and delicate, or dark and oily, for example.

Some people prefer not to eat fish because of the smell and the bones. It is always possible to have fish filleted, although cooking with the bones can mean a better flavor, and really fresh fish does not have an unpleasant smell. It smells of the sea.

Ideally, fish should be eaten within 48 hours of being caught, sooner if possible. Fish does not store. If planning to eat raw fish, it must be very fresh. There are three simple guidelines to recognizing whether or not a fish is fresh: it will have bright eyes, be firm to touch, and smell of the sea. Fish must always be cleaned and gutted before cooking or eating, and it may need scaling. Fish does cook quickly and it is easy to overcook: it will turn opaque when just done.

The many different types of fish have various different qualities: delicate, meaty, firm-fleshed, oily, soft-flesh, flaky, and so on. Each type of fish will take additional flavorings in its own ways. It is a case of knowing both the fish and the chosen accompaniments before attempting to combine them. This variety is part of the beauty of fish: it can take sweet and sour, herbs and spices, rice, noodles, pasta and potatoes, frying, steaming or braising. What is more, fish is highly nutritious, rich in protein, minerals and vitamins.

"Most of the Southeast Asian countries are seafood oriented. They are not in the middle of the desert, there is always a cold store, and there are a lot of appealing seafood dishes."

Barney Brown, chef at Betelnut

"I think when you eat a piece of fish you feel better. Depending on the time of day and how hungry you are and other things, personally I feel better after eating a piece of fish. I don't feel as bloated or overstuffed."

Kirk Webber, chef at Cafe Kati

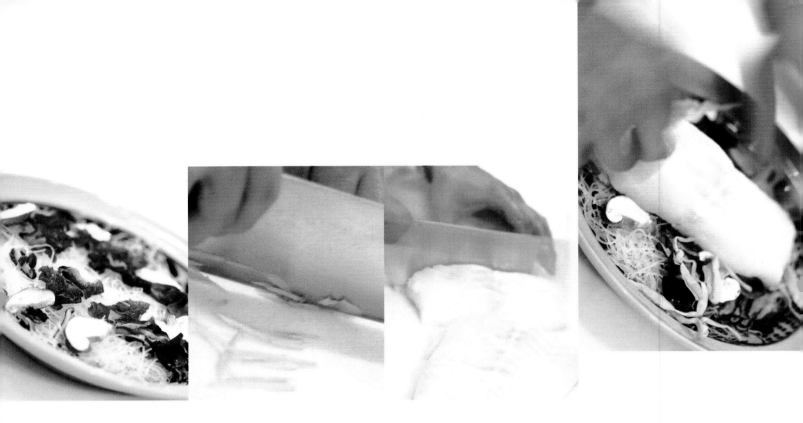

Steamed Sea Bass

1. Soak the lily buds, wood ears, glass noodles and shiitake mushrooms in hot water for 30 minutes. Rinse well and squeeze dry.

2. Trim off the hard knobs from the wood ears, then cut into small pieces. Discard the stems from the shiitake mushrooms, then cut across into ¼-inch-thick slices.

3. Heat the oil in a small saucepan, then add the chopped shallot. Fry until golden brown and set aside.

4. In a small bowl, combine the soy sauce, measured water and sugar until mixed well. Stir in the shallot and set aside.

5. Arrange the lily buds, wood ears, noodles and shiitake mushrooms in a deep serving dish that will fit in your steamer. Place the fish on top of the bed of noodles.

6. Pour the oil, shallot and soy mixture over the fish. Sprinkle with a little salt and pepper and scatter the ginger over the fish.

7. Bring at least 2 inches water to a boil in a large pan or wok, then put the dish of fish into a steamer and place the steamer in the pan. Steam over high heat for about 30 minutes, or until just cooked through. Do not open the steamer to check before about 20 minutes, but make sure that the water in the wok does not boil away. Serve with rice.

Serves 4

Charles Phan at The Slanted Door

20 dried lily buds

2 ounces wood ear mushrooms

1 ounce glass noodles (mung bean threads)

6 dried shiitake mushrooms

2 tablespoons vegetable oil

½ shallot, finely chopped

2 tablespoons light soy sauce

½ cup water

½ tablespoon sugar

10-ounce sea bass fillet

salt and pepper, to taste

1 tablespoon finely julienned ginger root

Seaweed Jelly
of Pink Seafood and Lime

1. Cook all the seafood very gently with the lime juice in a little simmering salted water. Remove from the heat, drain well and then chill the seafood thoroughly.

2. Divide the seafood, lime zest, chili pepper, cilantro, mushrooms and seaweed among six small Chinese soup bowls, arranging them decoratively in the bowls.

3. Make the jelly. Put the gelatin in the measured water in a saucepan for a few minutes until soft. Place the pan over low heat to dissolve the gelatin, swirling the liquid around in the pan. Stir in the lime juice and fish sauce and check for seasoning.

4. Allow the jelly mixture to cool slightly, then divide the jelly among the soup bowls. Chill until set firm.

5. Serve the jelly with a little wasabi on the side.

Serves 6

Michael Lee-Richards at Michael's

6 shucked oysters

6 large shrimp, peeled and deveined

3 mussels, shelved and halved horizontally

3 ounces sliced smoked salmon, cut into
   6 pieces and rolled

3 tablespoons shredded squid (about 3 ounces)

grated zest and juice of 1 lime

½ red chili pepper, seeded and finely
   shredded

12 cilantro leaves

1 ounce morel mushrooms

walnut-size clump of arame seaweed
   (or similar), soaked in water for 15 minutes

wasabi, to serve

Jelly

1 tablespoon unflavored gelatin

2 cups water

1 tablespoon lime juice

2 tablespoons fish sauce

"Fish has become more popular because it is such a light dish and is quick to prepare."

Michael Lee-Richards, chef at Michael's

Peppered Oysters
Rolled in Pastry with Five-flavor Vinaigrette

24 shucked oysters with their liquor

1 tablespoon olive oil

2 tablespoons finely chopped shallots

4 sheets puff pastry

oil for deep-frying (optional)

1 egg, lightly beaten with a pinch salt

salad greens (optional)

salt and pepper, to taste

Five-flavor Vinaigrette

2 tablespoons olive oil

1 tablespoon finely chopped ginger root

1 garlic clove, finely chopped

1 red chili pepper, seeded and finely
   chopped

1 tablespoon chopped cilantro

1 tablespoon tomato paste

1 tablespoon soy sauce

1 tablespoon white wine vinegar

1 tablespoon sesame oil

1 teaspoon sugar

1. Finely chop and then drain the oysters, reserving all the juice.

2. Heat the oil in a sauté pan. Add the shallots and cook, stirring, for a few minutes until lightly browned. Add the oyster juice to the pan and simmer until reduced to barely a glaze.

3. Remove the pan from the heat, stir in the oysters and season well with salt and pepper. Transfer to a shallow dish and then cool quickly in the refrigerator.

4. Cut the pastry into 2-inch rounds. Spoon a little of the cooled oyster mixture into the center of each piece of pastry and fold the pastry over the filling, sealing the edges with dampened fingers. Chill the small parcels in the refrigerator for 10 minutes.

5. Preheat the oven to 350°F. Alternatively, heat some oil in a deep-fat fryer to 350°F, or until a cube of bread browns in 30 seconds.

6. To bake the parcels, glaze the tops with the beaten egg, transfer to a baking sheet and bake in the oven for 10–12 minutes, until golden brown. If you prefer, fry the chilled parcels in the hot oil until golden and puffed. Drain on paper towels, keep warm in a low oven, then dust with salt and pepper.

7. While the parcels are baking, make the vinaigrette. Heat the oil in a small pan. Stir in the ginger, garlic and chili pepper and cook together for 2 minutes. Add the remaining ingredients and stir well to combine. Remove the pan from the heat and set aside for a moment.

8. To serve, either pile a few of the parcels in some salad greens (if using) on individual plates and drizzle with the vinaigrette, or serve them as a canapé with drinks.

Serves 8

Michael Lee-Richards at Michael's

'My fish guy is right on the wharf there. When the boats come in, he calls me and says that he's just got halibut in.'

Kirk Webber, chef at Cafe Kati

"Food and eating always have an impact on any culture, but I am sure there are still many people who only see food as fuel to keep their engines running, so they can tear off to their next appointment or whatever. It's a shame, because they miss out on some of the best social interaction of the day. There's nothing better than sitting around the table, sharing food and time with family and friends."

Michael Lee-Richards, chef at Michael's

Roast Monkfish
with Red Curry Sabayon and Gazpacho Hash

1. Make the sabayon. Whisk the egg yolks together with the wine in a stainless steel bowl. Cook, stirring, over a pan of gently boiling water until the mixture is thick and frothy, about 8 minutes.

2. Turn the heat off, but leave the bowl over the pan to keep warm. Stir in the curry paste, olive oil, lemon juice and the sugar, to taste. Season to taste with salt and pepper. Keep warm, stirring occasionally.

3. Make the hash. Cook the potatoes, unpeeled, in boiling water until soft. Drain well, then return to the pan and mash them roughly.

4. Stir in the remaining hash ingredients, season well with salt and pepper and keep warm.

5. Preheat the oven to 350°F. Brush the fish with the oil and season well with salt and pepper.

6. Place the fish in a roasting pan and cook for 10–15 minutes or until almost cooked. Transfer to a flameproof platter.

7. Preheat the broiler. Liberally pour most of the sabayon over the fish and place under the hot broiler until golden. You can also brown the dish using a blowtorch.

8. To serve, spoon some of the hash onto the center of each of six plates. Place a portion of fish over the hash and pour the remaining sabayon into a small jug for serving on the side.

Serves 6

Michael Lee-Richards at Michael's

Red Curry Sabayon

5 egg yolks

2 tablespoons white wine

1 heaped teaspoon red curry paste

2 tablespoons olive oil

juice of 1 lemon

sugar, to taste

salt and pepper, to taste

Gazpacho Hash

6 medium potatoes

2 tomatoes, peeled, seeded and diced

1 cucumber, peeled, seeded and diced

1 tablespoon finely chopped parsley

1 garlic clove, finely chopped

1 small red onion, finely chopped

salt and pepper, to taste

For the Monkfish

2 pounds monkfish

oil for brushing

salt and pepper, to taste

Fresh Tuna Rolls
with Scallops and Ginger

1. In a shallow dish, toss the tuna and scallops with the oil, ginger and lemon juice. Leave to rest for 15 minutes.

2. In a small bowl, blend the wasabi with the butter and salt.

3. Cut the crusts from the bread and cover the slices with a damp tea towel. Working with one slice at a time, spread the bread generously with the wasabi butter. Take care to get right to the edges.

4. Drain the tuna and scallops well. Lay a strip of the tuna and scallop mixture diagonally across the bread and top with some snow pea shoots so that some of the green is pointing out of the ends.

5. Roll up the bread carefully, taking care not to press too firmly. Cover the rolls with a damp tea towel until ready to serve.

Makes 20 rolls

Michael Lee-Richards at Michael's

7 ounces fresh tuna fillet, thinly sliced

5 ounces scallops, thinly sliced

2 tablespoons olive oil

1 teaspoon grated ginger root

juice of 1 lemon

2 teaspoons wasabi powder mixed to a paste
   with a little water

7 tablespoons butter, softened

¼ teaspoon salt

20 thin slices white bread

3½ ounces snow pea shoots

"When cutting raw fish it's very important to do so in one smooth cut and to use a very sharp knife. You should always pull the knife, never push it. Pulling the knife uses less pressure; it's also important to use the same amount of pressure throughout the cut."

Chef Suki, chef at Masons

"We take some Asian dishes and make them accessible."

Chris Benians, chef at The Collection

1. Make the dipping sauce. In a food processor, finely chop the cucumber with the shallot, chili pepper and ginger. Add the remaining sauce ingredients and process until nearly smooth. If you want to use a blender, purée all the ingredients together.

2. Heat a wok until almost smoking. Add 1 teaspoon of oil and the bok choy and stir-fry for 2–3 minutes. Add the soy sauce and cook for 30 seconds longer. Transfer to a bowl and allow to cool.

3. Add the crab and alfalfa to the bok choy and toss to mix.

4. Working with one spring roll wrapper at a time, lay the wrapper on the work surface and brush the beaten egg along three of the edges. Lay a little of the crab mixture along the fourth edge, then roll up the wrapper to make a long, thin spring roll about finger thickness.

5. Heat the oil in the wok to 350–375°F, or until a cube of bread browns in 30 seconds. Fry the spring rolls in batches until golden brown. Allow to drain on paper towels. Serve with a bowl of the cucumber dipping sauce.

Serves 6

Chris Benians and Cass Titcombe at The Collection

light flavorless oil for frying
1 bok choy, julienned
1 tablespoon soy sauce
8 ounces cooked crabmeat
1–2 ounces alfalfa sprouts
1 package spring roll wrappers
1 egg, lightly beaten

Dipping Sauce
1 small cucumber
1 shallot
1 red chili pepper, seeded
2 tablespoons pickled ginger
1 tablespoon fish sauce
1 tablespoon sushi vinegar (page 150)
handful of cilantro leaves
juice of ½ lime and ½ lemon

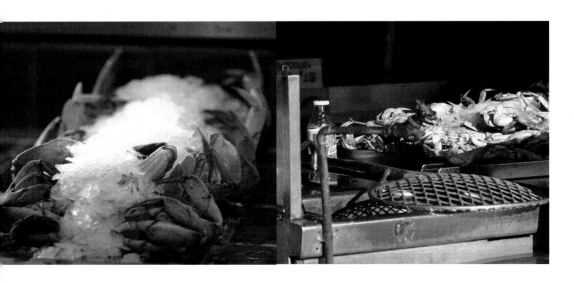

Crab Spring Rolls

Lobster and Salmon Soup

1. Combine all the soup base ingredients together in a large stockpot and cover with the measured water. Bring to a boil, reduce the heat, partially cover and simmer for 1 hour. Strain through a fine sieve and reserve.

2. Bring a saucepan of salted water to the boil. Add the noodles and cook until barely done, about 2 minutes less than the package instructions.

3. Pour 2 quarts of stock soup base into a large saucepan. Add the mussels, clams and ginger and bring to a boil to open the mussel and clam shells. Remove from the heat, check for seasoning and add soy sauce and lime juice to taste. Stir in the green onions.

4. Divide the noodles among four or six large and wide soup bowls. Remove the mussels and clams from the soup and add them to the bowls of noodles, discarding any that have not opened. Divide the remaining ingredients among the soup bowls.

5. Bring the stock back to a boil, then ladle over the soup ingredients and serve at once.

Serves 4–6

Chris Benians and Cass Titcombe at The Collection

7 ounces buckwheat noodles

40 mussels, scrubbed clean

20 clams, scrubbed clean

1 ounce ginger root, peeled and cut into very thin strips

soy sauce, to taste

lime juice, to taste

1 bunch green onions, sliced

8 ounces salmon fillet, thinly sliced

4 ounces green beans, blanched

2 bok choy, each cut into quarters

2 ounces enoki mushrooms

⅓ ounce wakame, soaked in a little warm water and then drained

Soup Base

2–3 lobster shells

1 bunch green onions

1 fennel bulb, chopped

1 tablespoon chopped ginger root

2 garlic cloves, chopped

3–4 quarts water

> "A lot of people will now eat raw fish and they will eat this and that raw. Japanese food is fashionable to eat, so they think, 'Well I'm in.'"
>
> Chris Benians, chef at The Collection

Seared Tuna Sashimi
with Shiitake Salad

1. Roll the tuna loin in the five-spice powder to coat evenly. Heat a heavy frying pan until very hot. Add the tuna and sear for about 3 minutes, turning frequently to brown all over. Remove from the frying pan and allow to cool.

2. Mix all the dressing ingredients together in a small bowl.

3. Toss all the salad vegetables together and mix with the dressing.

4. Heat the oil to 325°F. Fry the lotus root until quite crisp, but not colored. Drain on paper towels. Skewer the fried lotus root slices with the pickled ginger slices onto small bamboo skewers.

5. Cut the tuna across into ⅛-inch-thick slices and divide among four plates. Mound the salad next to the tuna and accompany with a skewer of lotus root and ginger. Garnish each serving with wasabi and shiso leaves.

Serve 4

Chris Benians and Cass Titcombe at The Collection

MOOLI, LOTUS ROOT AND SHISO LEAVES

Mooli, a variety of Asian white radish, looks similar to a parsnip. It has a fresh, peppery taste, and if it is to be cooked, it should be salted for 30 minutes beforehand.

Lotus root is the underwater rhizome of the lotus flower. Related to the water lily, it has a sweet, crunchy texture and a lacelike appearance when sliced. Lotus root can be bought canned, although it is not as fresh tasting.

Shiso is commonly used in Japanese cookery. It is a herb related to basil and mint, with a flavor not unlike anise. Shiso comes in both red and green leaf varieties and is also known as the beefsteak plant.

7 ounces tuna fillet, in one piece

1 teaspoon five-spice powder

oil for deep-frying

4-inch piece lotus root, thinly sliced

¼ cup thinly sliced pickled ginger

Dressing

2 tablespoons soy sauce

1 teaspoon sesame oil

1 teaspoon sunflower oil

juice of 1 lime

Salad

8 fresh shiitake mushrooms, finely sliced

3 green onions, finely sliced

4 ounces mooli, peeled and shredded

½ cucumber, shredded

Garnish

1 teaspoon wasabi paste

1 bunch of shiso leaves

the
fast-food
effect

Most of us accept that the hamburger is fast food. In effect, so is so much else of what we eat.

Hamburgers and fast food do not have to be tasteless things that we wish we were not eating. They can, and should be, delicious and nutritious.

The demand for food to be delivered quickly stems from our lifestyles. Busy people with too much to do and not enough time need the most important thing in life quickly. Food is fuel.

To look at fast food in a different light is to recognize that the simplest (which often means quickest) of foods can be enhanced. A hamburger can be made with the finest quality beef and served with mouthwatering homemade relishes and pickles and the freshest of salads. Noodles are also quick, and can easily be stirred up into a delicious dish. Rice, too, is quick to cook. Both noodles and rice can carry sauces and a variety of meat, poultry, fish and vegetables. Eggs are also speedy cookers, and are easily enhanced by, say, some onions, ham and a tomato salsa.

Fast food need not be boring food. With the widening of the food spectrum seen in East-West food, fast food has the scope to become some of the best food we eat. So many foods and ideas picked up from all over the world require very little cooking to keep their natural qualities. Perhaps this is what is needed to make fast food real food.

"I think we are going to start seeing more exciting fast-food concepts."

Kirk Webber, chef at Cafe Kati

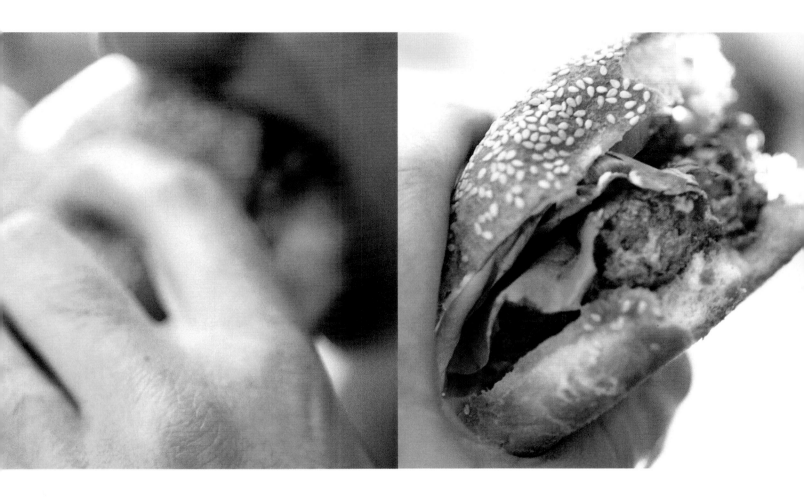

"We do get the food out quickly. Even when we're busy, the food does go out quickly. I think that's partly the impact of lifestyles; everybody expects everything faster."

Chris Benians, chef at The Collection

> "Fast food is here. It's a trend that's not going to stop, even though most chefs don't agree and don't like it. It's here and I hope it gets better, and I think it will, too."

Kirk Webber, chef at Cafe Kati

1. Cook the lobster in a large pan of boiling water, allow to cool, then remove the meat and dice it.

2. Heat the oil in a deep pan to 350–375°F, or until a cube of bread browns in 30 seconds. Fry the wonton wrappers until crisp, using a pair of tongs to help form them into the shape of taco shells. Remove and drain on paper towels.

3. Make the vinaigrette. Combine the first eight ingredients in a saucepan, bring to a boil and simmer for 15 minutes. Whisk in the cornstarch mixture while still on the heat. Remove from the heat, cool completely and strain. Stir in the chopped cilantro.

4. Mix together all the salad ingredients. Toss with enough spicy vinaigrette to lightly coat the salad mixture.

5. Place 2 tablespoons salad mixture at the bottom of each taco shell, then place 1 tablespoon of lobster meat on top and serve with wedges of cucumber.

Serves 4

Kirk Webber at Cafe Kati

TACOS

The most well-known and commonly found tacos are folded, deep-fried, crisp tortillas. Traditionally they have a spicy meat filling.

1 live lobster, 1–1½ pounds

oil for deep-frying

16 wonton wrappers

cucumber wedges, to garnish

Salad Mixture

1 cup shredded green papaya

1 romaine lettuce heart, shredded

⅔ cup shredded red cabbage

24 mint leaves, torn in half

1 bunch cilantro sprigs

Spicy Thai Vinaigrette

2 stalks lemongrass, chopped roughly

6 kaffir lime leaves (optional)

1 head of garlic, cut in half

1 tablespoon red chili paste

2 tablespoons fish sauce

1 cup lemon juice

1 cup rice wine vinegar

¼ cup sugar

½ tablespoon cornstarch dissolved in
   2 tablespoons water

1 bunch cilantro leaves, roughly chopped

Crispy Wonton Lobster Tacos
with Green Papayas and Mint

Steamed Water Omelet
with Carrot and Cilantro

1. Make the filling by combining all the ingredients in a bowl. Cover with plastic wrap and marinate for several hours in the refrigerator.

2. Make the omelet batter, using the eggs lightly beaten with the measured water and the herbs. Heat a nonstick crêpe pan. Melt the butter. Pour in a thin film of the batter and cook genty until set.

3. Turn the omelet out onto a work surface and cover with a damp tea towel. Repeat to make more omelets until all the batter is used.

4. Discard the lemongrass. Place some of the filling over each omelet and roll up to enclose the filling. Cut the rolls across into slices. Serve with a bowl of fish sauce or sweet chili sauce for dipping.

Serves 4 as a starter or 2 for lunch

Michael Lee-Richards at Michael's

Omelet

4 eggs

¼ cup water

1½–2 cups mixed herbs, chopped

2 tablespoons butter

fish sauce or sweet chili sauce, to serve

Filling

1½ cups grated carrots

2 garlic cloves, finely chopped

1 red chili pepper, seeded and finely chopped

1-inch piece ginger root, peeled and finely chopped

1 teaspoon brown sugar

1 stalk lemongrass, cut into pieces

juice of 3 limes or 1 lemon

2 teaspoons fish sauce

2 tablespoons torn cilantro leaves and finely chopped stems

2 tablespoons chopped unsalted raw peanuts

"Woks are great for fast, easy and tasty food, although it's not always necessary to do stir-fries. Soups can be made quickly and easily, and mussels, of course, take no time to cook."

Spicy Mussel Soup

4 cups chicken stock

2 garlic cloves

3 cilantro roots

3 black peppercorns, crushed

3 slices galangal root

6 kaffir lime leaves, julienned

3 stalks lemongrass, each cut into 3 pieces

4 tomatoes, cut into quarters and seeded

2½ pounds mussels, scrubbed clean

5 dried red chilies, crushed

3–4 tablespoons lime juice

3–4 tablespoons fish sauce

Garnish

3 tablespoons julienned cilantro leaves

3 tablespoons julienned Thai basil leaves

2 red chilies, julienned

1. Bring the chicken stock to the boil in a wok and simmer gently for 10 minutes.

2. Make a paste from the garlic, cilantro roots and peppercorns and add to the stock. Add the galangal, lime leaves, lemongrass, tomatoes and mussels and bring back to a boil.

3. Add the dried chilies. Season with the lime juice and fish sauce. Taste and adjust the seasoning if necessary. Discard any mussels that have not opened. Ladle the mussel soup into six bowls, and serve sprinkled with the julienne of herbs and chili.

Serves 4–6

Graham Harris at Cicada

"These fritters are incredibly quick to prepare if you have a food processor. A food processor is one of the best aids to fast food, as it cuts down your preparation time immensely. I serve these fritters either small as canapés, with a sweet chili sauce, or large, as you would a hamburger. Put them in a sourdough bun, topped with pickled cucumber and beets and lashings of tomato salsa; it's a real treat. The most time-consuming thing about this recipe is the assembling of the ingredients."

Duck, Cilantro,
Sweet Potato and Lime Fritters

3 large duck breasts, boned, skinned, fat and sinews removed, roughly chopped and refrigerated until needed

1 bunch cilantro, roughly chopped (try to get one with the roots intact and wash well)

8 kaffir lime leaves, finely shredded

4 garlic cloves

2 tablespoons finely grated ginger root

2 tablespoons fish sauce

2 teaspoons sesame seeds, toasted

2 eggs

2 green onions, finely sliced

about 1 cup finely grated sweet potato, excess moisture squeezed out

½ cup cornstarch, plus 3 tablespoons for coating

oil for brushing

1. Put all the ingredients except the eggs, green onions, sweet potato, cornstarch and oil in a food processor and purée until very finely chopped.

2. Add the remaining ingredients except the 3 tablespoons of cornstarch and the oil and process just until combined.

3. Divide the mixture into 6 handfuls and roll each into a ball. Coat them in the remaining cornstarch to cover lightly, then flatten to disks about ¾ inch thick.

4. Heat either a heavy frying pan or broiler and lightly brush the fritters with some cooking oil. Cook the fritters for about 3–4 minutes on each side or until golden and still slightly rare in the middle.

Makes 6 large fritters (or 18 canapé-size ones)

Peter Gordon at The Sugar Club

Chicken and Lettuce Rolls

3 garlic cloves, very finely chopped

⅓ cup very finely chopped ginger root

¼ cup soy sauce

1 skinless, boneless chicken breast

7 tablespoons white wine vinegar

½ cup sugar

7 tablespoons water

2 bird's eye chili peppers, 1 seeded and finely chopped and 1 left whole

1 carrot, julienned

1 head romaine lettuce

¼ cup fish sauce

juice of 1 lime

1 bunch green onions, julienned

2 tablespoons butter

1. In a small bowl, mix half the garlic and ginger together. Stir in 1 tablespoon of the soy sauce. Spread the mixture all over the chicken, cover and marinate in the refrigerator for at least 1 hour.

2. In a saucepan, combine the vinegar with three-quarters of the sugar, the measured water, the remaining garlic and ginger and the whole chili pepper. Bring the mixture to a boil, then remove from the heat and pour over the carrot in a shallow dish. Cover and leave to cool completely.

3. Separate the lettuce leaves and blanch them in boiling water for just about 30 seconds. Drain and transfer to ice water at once, to cool. Drain again and lay on tea towels to dry.

4. Make a dipping sauce. In a small bowl, combine the remaining soy sauce with the fish sauce, lime juice, chopped chili pepper and remaining sugar. Leave to allow the flavors to blend.

5. Pan-fry the chicken breast in the butter, in a very hot sauté pan until golden and cooked through, turning once. Remove from the pan and leave to cool.

6. Assemble the rolls. Drain all the liquid from the carrots and discard the chili pepper. Cut the chicken breast across into very thin slices. Cut out the stems that run down the middle of the lettuce leaves by cutting the leaves lengthwise in half. At one end, lay 1–2 slices of chicken on top of each of the lettuce leaf strips, top with a little green onion and some carrots. Roll up the leaves like short fat cigars. Serve the rolls with the dipping sauce.

Serves 6

Chris Benians and Cass Titcombe at The Collection

index

acknowledgments

There are so many people to thank in the making of this book. Someone's sure to be left out, so we thank you now!

In particular thanks must go to all the chefs who generously gave up their time and allowed us to overrun their restaurants. Thanks to Charles Phan and all at The Slanted Door, to Kirk Webber and all at Cafe Kati, to Chef Suki and his chefs, to Giselle Bonilla, to Barney Brown and all at Betelnut, to Peter Gordon and all at The Sugar Club, to Chris Benians, Cass Titcombe and all at The Collection. Thanks also to the vendors and shoppers at the various markets we visited, to Costarella's, the Japan Centre, and to everyone else who allowed us to photograph them.

Many thanks as well to the chefs and others who contributed but whom we could not visit: Michael Lee-Richards and Tina Duncan, Graham Harris and Stanislaus Soares.

Huge thanks must go to Carol and Bruce Mitchell for making us so welcome, to Jeremy "the packhorse" Leach, and to Richard for all his help and, well, everything.

Notes

1. Look for the more unusual ingredients in Chinese, Japanese, and Southeast Asian markets and in the international foods section of well-stocked supermarkets.
2. Eggs should be large unless otherwise stated.
3. Use whole milk unless otherwise stated.
4. Pepper should be freshly ground black pepper unless otherwise stated.
5. Fresh herbs should be used unless otherwise stated. If unavailable, use dried herbs as an alternative, but halve the quantities stated.
6. Ovens should be preheated to the specified temperature. If using a fan-assisted oven, follow the manufacturer's instructions for adjusting the time and the temperature.